IN PONDS AND STREAMS

Books by Margaret Waring Buck

IN WOODS AND FIELDS

IN YARDS AND GARDENS

IN PONDS AND STREAMS

IN PONDS AND STREAMS

Written and illustrated by

MARGARET WARING BUCK

New York   **ABINGDON PRESS**   *Nashville*

FOR HENRY
who found and caught
live models for many of the pictures

THIS BOOK is for boys and girls and others who feel the lure of ponds and streams. It is fun to find the different kinds of plants and to watch the creatures that live in, on, and around small bodies of water. This becomes even more interesting when we know what to look for and how to identify what we find. The locale of IN PONDS AND STREAMS is the northeastern United States but much that is in it applies equally to many other parts of this country and to southern Canada. Descriptions and pictures are based on firsthand exploration and extensive research. Young friends, especially Henry Levinson, have assisted by bringing in many models, both living and dead. In addition, each section has been checked by leading authorities in the special fields.

The author wishes to express her thanks and indebtedness to these naturalists connected with The American Museum of Natural History: Mont A. Cazier, Chairman and Curator, and John C. Pallister, Research Associate, Department of Insects; John T. Nichols, Curator Emeritus, and Francesca R. La Monte, Associate Curator, Department of Fishes; C. M. Bogert, Curator, Department of Amphibians and Reptiles; Libbie H. Hyman, Research Associate in Invertebrates; John T. Zimmer, Curator, Department of Birds; T. D. Carter, Assistant Curator, Department of Mammals. She is also indebted to these Smithsonian Institution experts: Edward A. Chapin, Acting Head Curator, Department of Zoology; Fenner A. Chase, Jr., Curator, Division of Marine Invertebrates; Joseph P. E. Morrison, Division of Mollusks; and to Marvin Clinton Meyer, Associate Professor, Department of Zoology, University of Maine; and to D. P. Rogers, Curator, The New York Botanical Garden.

CONTENTS

IN PONDS AND STREAMS

Every time you go exploring near water you will discover something new. For all ponds, streams, and other bodies of fresh water have many things living and growing in and around them.
Let's find out about some of these plants and creatures.

SMALL FLOWERING PLANTS

Along the banks of most ponds and streams are many flowering plants. The ones shown on this page bloom in spring and early summer.

The trout lily (adder's-tongue or dogtooth violet) blooms in April and May. Each flower stem grows from 5 to 10 inches high. It is topped by one nodding flower which is yellow inside and greenish on the outside. The long leaves which grow from the bulb are mottled green and reddish-brown. Less common are trout lilies with white or lavender flowers.

The swamp buttercup has larger flowers and leaves than the common buttercup. It grows from 1 to 2 feet high and blooms in wet places from April to July.

The marsh marigold (cowslip) has golden yellow flowers much like the swamp buttercup. It blooms at the same time and grows to about the same height. You can tell the two plants apart by their leaves. The marsh marigold has broad, heart-shaped leaves. In spring these young leaves and stems make good cooked greens.

The familiar small blue flowers of the forget-me-not grow wild beside many brooks and in moist meadows. The flowers bloom from May to July and later. They bloom along the tops of the stems, which are from 6 to 18 inches high.

TROUT LILY   SWAMP BUTTERCUP   MARSH MARIGOLD   FORGET-ME-NOT

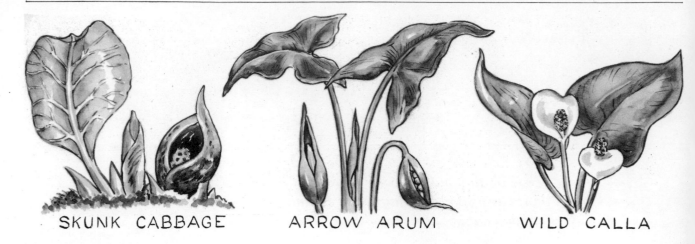

SKUNK CABBAGE   ARROW ARUM   WILD CALLA

LARGE-LEAVED PLANTS

Clumps of plants with arrow- or heart-shaped leaves grow at the edge of ponds and streams.

Skunk cabbage has heart-shaped leaves with coarse veins. By late spring the leaves are 2 or more feet high. The flowers come very early in spring, before the leaves have unrolled. They are on a thick spike enclosed in a mottled green, purple, and red hood.

Arrow arum has arrow-shaped leaves which grow from 1 to 2 feet high. In May and June it has a flower spike enclosed in a long green hood. After the flower fades, the stem curves downward so that the hood, which is then short, fat, and filled with green berries, is in the water.

The wild calla, or water arum, which blooms at the same time as the arrow arum, has a white open hood around its flower spike. It grows from 5 to 10 inches high in cool, shady bogs, and has heart-shaped leaves.

Arrowhead has small white flowers in summer. Each flower has three petals and grows in a group of three. The leaves vary in different species; some are arrow shaped, broad or narrow; some are grass-like. The broad-leaved kind grows to 2 feet high.

The water plantain has tiny three-petaled white or pink flowers on many-branching stems. It blooms in summer and grows from 1 to 3 feet high. The leaves are heart shaped, deeply veined.

Pickerelweed has spikes of blue-violet flowers from June to October. The leaves are large and heart shaped. The plant grows to 3 feet high.

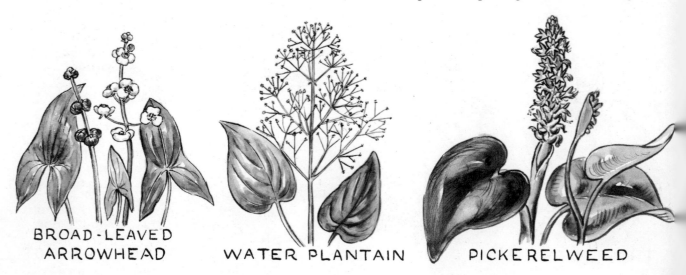

BROAD-LEAVED ARROWHEAD   WATER PLANTAIN   PICKERELWEED

GOLDEN CLUB   SWEET FLAG   (Narrow) BLUE FLAG (Larger)

OBLONG- AND NARROW-LEAVED PLANTS

Golden club grows in ponds and swamps. The oblong leaves either stand erect or float on the water. In April and May there are spikes of golden flowers at the top of thick 2-foot-long stems.

The sweet flag (calamus) is related to the golden club. Its greenish-yellow flowers grow from May to July in long spikes from the side of leaflike stems. The leaves, which grow from 2 to 6 feet tall, are narrow and pointed. The roots are made into candy and are used as medicine.

The larger blue flag has narrow leaves like the garden iris. It blooms from May to July and has blue-violet flowers with white centers. The narrow blue flag has grasslike leaves and slender blue-violet flowers in May and June.

WATER LILIES

Water lilies have large rounded leaves which float on the water or stand above it. They cover large areas in many ponds and sluggish streams.

From April to September the yellow pond lily (spatterdock) has yellow cup-shaped flowers which measure from 1½ to 3 inches across. The large heart-shaped leaves stand above the water.

In June the sweet-scented white water lily begins to bloom. The flowers, from 3 to 6 inches across, open early in the morning and close at night. The round leaves float on the water.

The large leaves and pale yellow flowers of the American lotus grow on long stems which lift them above the water. Indians eat their nutlike seeds as well as their roots and young shoots.

YELLOW POND LILY   WHITE WATER LILY   AMERICAN LOTUS

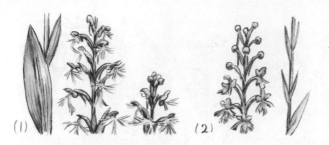

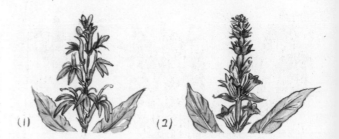

FRINGED ORCHID: 1) GREEN; 2) PURPLE

1) Fringed greenish-yellow flowers grow along a 1- to 2-foot stem in June and July. 2) Light or deep purple flowers on 1- to 3-foot stems in July and August. Other kinds of fringed orchids have yellow or white flowers.

1) CARDINAL FLOWER; 2) BLUE LOBELIA

1) Spikes of scarlet flowers in summer with deep tubes which hummingbirds like. 2) Blue, heavier flowers from July to October. Both plants grow from 2 to 3 feet or more high along the edge of wooded streams.

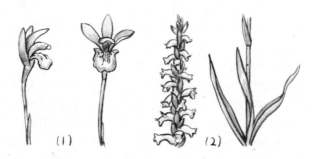

1) ARETHUSA; 2) NODDING LADIES' TRESSES

1) A single pink flower grows on a 5- to 10-inch leafless stem in May and June. 2) Tiny, fragrant white flowers twine around the stem in later summer. It grows from 6 to 24 inches high.

JEWELWEED (TOUCH-ME-NOT)

This plant grows from 2 to 3 feet high in wet places. It blooms in summer and fall. One kind has pale yellow flowers; the other kind has spotted orange flowers. The long, pale green seed pods snap open at a touch.

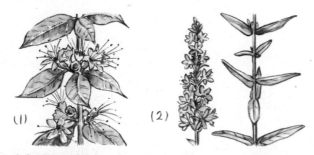

LOOSESTRIFE: 1) SWAMP; 2) PURPLE

1) Purple flowers in clusters along the stem between the leaves in summer. It grows from 3 to 10 feet high. 2) Purple flowers in a spike at top of stem in summer. It grows from 2 to 3 feet high and is often planted in gardens.

TURTLEHEAD

From July to September this plant has white or pinkish flowers about an inch long, which resemble a turtle's head. The long, deep green leaves grow in pairs along a four-sided stem. The plant grows from 1 to 3 feet high.

PONDWEEDS

1) Floating-leaved pondweed has heart-shaped leaves above and narrow leaves under water. Flowers and seeds are in spikes above water. 2) Sago pondweed has narrow, bristle-like leaves. 3) Ruffle-leaved pondweed has thin brown leaves.

1) HORNWORT; 2) BLADDERWORT

Both plants have long rootless stems which float under the water. 1) Threadlike leaves in groups along the stem. 2) Finely divided leaves with bladders which are traps to catch tiny water animals. Bladderwort has yellow flowers above water.

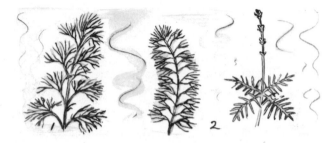

DUCKWEEDS

Float in masses on still water. 1) Ivy-leaved duckweed has narrow leaves ½ inch long. 2) Larger duckweed has leaves 1/3 inch long which are purple below. 3) Lesser duckweed leaves are ¼ inch long. 4) Watermeal is tiny and rootless.

1) CABOMBA; 2) WATER MILFOIL

Both plants are used in aquariums. 1) Feathery fan-shaped leaves on long stems either floating or rooted. 2) Finely divided leaves on long trailing stems. Milfoil has small purple flowers on a spike above the water.

1) WATERWEED (ELODEA); 2) TAPE GRASS

1) Thin, papery green leaves in groups of three or more along a long floating stem. 2) Ribbon-like leaves which grow to 3 feet long and tiny green seed-bearing flowers which float on springy stems.

1) WATER BUTTERCUP; 2) WATER CLOVER

1) Weak stems 1 foot or longer and threadlike spreading leaves. The white flowers stand above the water in summer. 2) An underwater fern with fronds like a four-leaf clover.

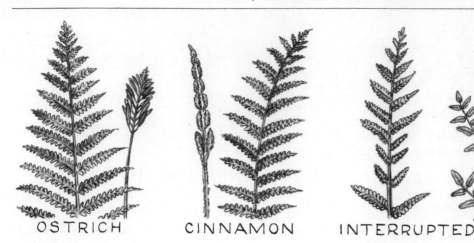

OSTRICH   CINNAMON   INTERRUPTED   ROYAL

FERNS

These beautiful ferns grow in wet places and have fronds that sometimes are 5 feet long.

The ostrich fern has wide feathery fronds and brown spore-bearing plumes which rise from its center in late summer and autumn.

The cinnamon fern has narrower fronds than the ostrich fern. In early summer its spores are like thick clusters of brown beads along the top of its stems.

The interrupted fern in spring has pairs of spore-bearing leaflets near the center of the frond.

The royal fern has wider spaces between its leaflets than the other ferns shown on this page. In spring its spores grow in beady clusters at the top of its stem.

RUSHES AND REEDS

These plants grow in swamps and at the edge of ponds. They have long narrow leaves.

Cattails have a flower spike which is brown below and yellow with pollen above. In summer the pollen blows away, leaving the brown part which holds the fluffy seeds.

Burreed flowers grow in balls along the stem, the smaller, fluffy heads being above the larger balls which hold the seeds, or nutlets.

American bulrushes have tall stems with clusters of small black nutlets which water birds like to eat. Their roots form thick mats.

Reeds have silky, ornamental flower heads which do not form many seeds; the plants are spread by their long, strong roots.

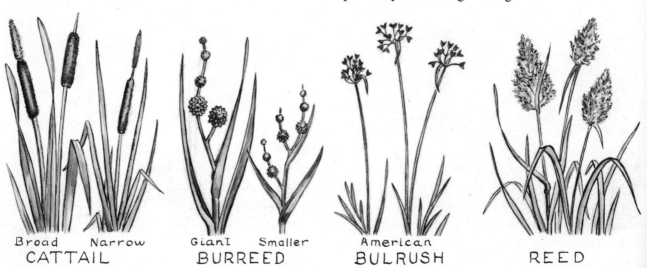

Broad   Narrow   Giant   Smaller   American
CATTAIL   BURREED   BULRUSH   REED

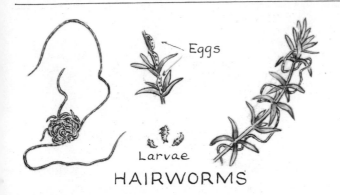
HAIRWORMS

WATER WORMS

Ponds and streams are full of different kinds of animal life.

Hairworms (hair snakes) are reddish-brown, threadlike worms, from 1 to 2 feet long. They twist around water plants or coil in tangled masses at the bottom of a pond. Starting life as eggs in strings of jelly attached to water plants, they hatch into squirming larvae. The larvae find water insects and bore into their bodies. Some larvae may be eaten by grasshoppers and crickets. The larvae live in the insects until they are grown. Then they return to water, if possible, to mate and lay eggs.

Flatworms are small worms which glide along on plants or stones in cool water. Most of them feed on animal juices which they suck through a tube on the underside of their body. Each worm is both male and female. It lays several eggs in a round capsule at intervals during the breeding season. Flatworms also increase by dividing in the middle. One kind, the chain flatworm, sometimes is made up of two, four, or more newly-divided worms attached together. It is transparent, only ¼ inch long, and is found on water plants.

The small black flatworm and the spotted one are ¼ inch long. The large black flatworm grows to 1 inch in length; the white one may be longer.

Leeches are wormlike creatures which usually live in the shallow water of ponds, streams, and swamps. They have a sucking mouth at one end and at the other end a suction cup with which they cling to stones, sticks, or animals. They feed by sucking blood from water creatures. The smaller leeches choose turtles, worms, snails, etc. The large leeches cling to wading animals. After the leech has had its fill, it usually drops off. It may not feed again for weeks or months. Leeches increase by laying eggs, either in hard-shelled cocoons attached to some support or in masses attached to themselves.

Turtle leeches carry their eggs and, for a time, their young on the underside of their bodies. During this time they feed on snails and insects instead of attaching themselves to turtles. In color they are 1) brown with yellowish lines and spots; 2) greenish with yellow blotches. They grow to 2 inches or more in length.

The worm leech is brown or black and grows from 1 to 4 inches long.

The American medicinal leech (3 to 6 inches long) is dull greenish with red and black spots on the back, orange underneath.

The horse leech (4 or 5 inches or longer) is greenish-brown with black spots on the back.

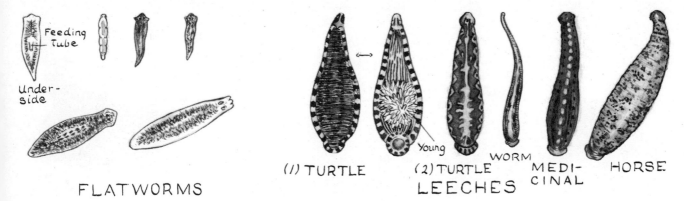
FLATWORMS
(1) TURTLE   (2) TURTLE   WORM   MEDI-   HORSE
LEECHES   CINAL

TADPOLE SNAIL   LARGE WHEEL SNAILS   SMALL HAIRY   LIMPETS   SMALL POND SNAIL

SNAILS

Fresh-water snails have spiral shells of different shapes and sizes. The body of the snail is twisted like its shell and usually fills it. The bottom of the body is flat and forms the foot on which the snail glides. The head has two feelers (tentacles) with the eyes at the base of the feelers. The mouth is on the underside and has a rough, filelike tongue. With this the snail scrapes up its food — the leaves of water plants and pond scum. Some snails are both male and female; some are one or the other. Most of them mate, but some increase without mating. Most of them lay eggs in small masses of jelly on something in the water.

The tadpole, wheel, and pond snails, and limpets get oxygen from air drawn into a lung sac.

The tadpole snail has a thin, shiny brown shell with a left-hand twist, about ½ inch long. It glides about very actively on its pointed foot.

Wheel snails have brown shells that are flattened on each side. The large kind is about 1 inch across. The small wheel and the hairy kind are not more than ⅕ or ¼ inch wide and are very flat.

Limpets are snails, less than ¼ inch long, with shells like low cones. They crawl on such things as stones, sticks, or plants. For breathing they have a gill as well as a lung sac.

The pond snails have a light or a dark brown shell with a long spire twisted upward to the right. They have a short, wide foot and short, triangular feelers. The small pond snail grows to a little more than 1 inch long; the great pond snail grows to over 2 inches.

The ridged wheel, the green, and the rounded pond snails get oxygen from the water through gills. Each has an operculum, which is a horny plate or door that closes the opening of the shell.

The tiny brown or greenish shell of the ridged wheel snail is only ¼ inch across. A feathery gill stands out from the shell when the snail moves.

The green snail burrows in sand, clay, or mud in shallow streams. Its shell is greenish with brown markings and grows to about 1½ inches long. The oldest (top) whorls are usually worn off. These snails bear their young alive.

The large rounded pond snail has a dark brown shell which grows to over 2 inches long. The females bear the young alive, often by the dozen.

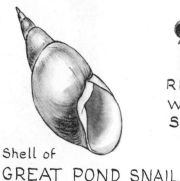

Shell of GREAT POND SNAIL   RIDGED WHEEL SNAIL   GREEN SNAIL

ROUNDED (Operculum) POND SNAIL

PILL CLAMS

FINGERNAIL CLAMS

LARGE MUSSEL

CLAMS

Clams of different shapes and sizes live in fresh water. The shell of each has a matching right- and left-hand half which are held together by a hinge at the top. Usually the shell halves are slightly open to let the foot stick out near one end and the siphons, or "necks," at the other end.

The clam moves by pulling itself along with its foot. It eats the tiny bits of living matter in the water which enter through its siphons. It breathes the oxygen in the water which is filtered through its gills.

Tiny pill clams and fingernail clams live in the sand and mud of ponds, lakes, and rivers. Sometimes they use their long tongue-like foot to crawl up water plants. Each clam is both male and female. During the year it produces a few eggs at a time. It holds the eggs in its gills until the young hatch and grow enough to be independent.

Pill clams have only one siphon. Their one-sided white, yellow, or greenish shells are only ⅛ to ⅜ of an inch long when full grown. Fingernail clams have two siphons and evenly balanced, light brown, yellow, or white shells ½ or ¾ inch long.

Large clams, or mussels, live in the mud of ponds and slow-moving streams. These mussels are either male or female. The female produces thousands of eggs which she holds in her gills until they are fertilized and hatched. When the young leave the parent they are not able to live independently. They must clamp onto fish and live on them for several weeks. Each kind of young mussel chooses a special kind of fish. The fat mucket chooses bass; the paper-shell mussel chooses sunfish.

The fat mucket has a light or a dark green shell about 4 inches long by 2 inches wide. The lining of the shell is mother-of-pearl and is used to make buttons and ornaments.

Pearl mussel shells are from 3 to 4 inches long, dark on the outside, pearly white or purple inside.

Paper-shell mussels have thin, shiny, greenish-brown shells with the pearly lining dull white or pinkish. They grow to be about 4 inches long.

FAT MUCKET

PEARL MUSSEL

PAPER-SHELL MUSSEL

SCUDS

WATER SOW BUG

Underside   Brood Pouch

SHELLFISHES (CRUSTACEANS)

The bodies of these water creatures are covered with shells divided into segments.

Scuds (amphipods) have narrow bodies and arched backs. They are gray, brown, or greenish. Of the two common kinds which live in ponds in the eastern states, one grows to ½ inch and the other to 1 inch long. With their dozen or more sets of legs they can climb, jump, walk, swim, feel, and grasp. Usually they swim on one side, waving their legs in the water. Scuds eat water plants and dead animal and plant matter.

In warm weather scuds increase fast; each female lays about twenty eggs every ten days or so. She carries the young in a brood pouch under her body until she is ready to have more eggs. In a little over a month, the young may lay eggs.

The water sow bug is a crustacean, not a bug. It is flat, gray, and a little over ½ inch long. On its seven pairs of legs it crawls at the bottom of a pond or puddle among the plants and dead leaves that it eats. The female has a whitish brood pouch under her body that is full of eggs or young during most of the warm weather. She lays eggs every five or six weeks and carries the young about a month.

Crayfish live along the edge of streams. They hide under rocks or in tunnels that they build in the banks or on moist land. The tunnels have little walls, or turrets, around their top entrance.

Crayfish are from 3 to 5 inches long and are grayish-brown, sometimes with tinges of red on the tail and legs. The first pair of legs are strong claws. With these the crayfish catches the small fish and insects that it eats, along with dead plant and animal matter. The other four pairs of legs are for walking. Hanging from the tail segments are the swimmerets with which the crayfish swims.

The female uses her swimmerets also to hold her eggs and young. She fastens the eggs with a kind of glue. When the young hatch, after seven or eight weeks, they cling to the swimmerets for a few days. The common crayfish may have eggs or young throughout the year. The chimney crayfish, which makes tunnels, mates in fall and lays eggs in spring. The usual life of a crayfish is less than twenty months, although some may live longer.

Eggs

CRAYFISH

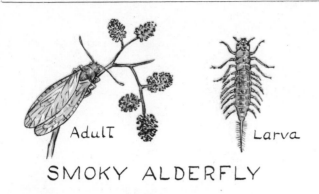

SMOKY ALDERFLY

Adult

Larva

INSECTS

Some insects live in water all their lives. Others start life in water and end it on land. Water insects go through the same stages that land insects do. They start as eggs which hatch into larvae or nymphs. When full grown, the larvae form pupae from which the adult winged insects emerge. Some insects skip the pupal stage. The three insects shown on this page spend their larval stage in water and their adult stage in air.

Smoky alderflies are so named because they are often seen around alder bushes. They are awkward fliers, about an inch long. The females lay their brown eggs in flat masses on leaves, branches, or stones above moving water. The larvae, which hatch from the eggs, fall into the water and burrow into the mud or sand at the bottom. They are brown and have seven pairs of fringed gills on the sides and a tail gill. They eat one another as well as other insects. When full grown, they are about an inch long. Then they crawl out on land, become

pupae, and change into gauzy-winged alderflies.

The dobson-fly is a fierce-looking creature in both adult and larval forms. The adult, which sometimes flies around lights, has four finely-veined gauzy wings with a spread of 5 inches. The male has long hornlike jaws with which it grasps the female. Her jaws are shorter but better able to bite. She lays chalky white masses of eggs (up to two thousand of them in a mass 1 inch across) on stones or other support over swift water. The newly hatched larvae fall into the water, where they live for two or three years. The larvae are called hellgrammites. They have strong jaws with which they capture the tiny fish, insects, and other creatures that they eat. In late spring the mature hellgrammites take to the land to form pupae and change into the short-lived dobson-flies.

The fish-fly is brown with yellow streaks and has grayish-brown lacy wings spotted with white, with a spread of over 3 inches. The female lays masses of reddish-brown eggs (from one to two thousand eggs in a mass) on leaves or branches over quiet water. The newly-hatched larvae fall into the water, where they live on insects and grow to be a little over an inch long. They have brown bodies with hairlike projections on the sides and tail, and shiny black heads. In late spring the larvae crawl upon a bank to form pupae under a stone, log, or in the earth. The adult fish-fly which emerges lives only a short time and is not often seen as it usually flies at dusk.

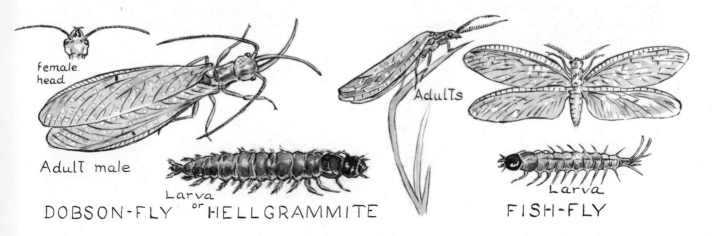

female head

Adult male

DOBSON-FLY or HELLGRAMMITE

Larva

Adults

FISH-FLY

Larva

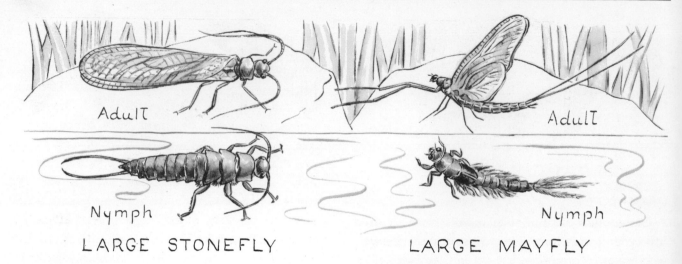

LARGE STONEFLY   LARGE MAYFLY

STONEFLIES

Stoneflies have grayish-brown or green bodies and four clear, veined wings which they fold flat against their backs when at rest. There are a number of different kinds of stoneflies. They vary in size from ½ to 2½ inches long. They fly near water and lay their eggs in the water. The eggs hatch into nymphs which have rather flat brown or greenish bodies and two thin tails. Their gills are under their bodies in the form of tufts or filaments. Their feet have two claws. The nymphs live under stones and rubbish at the bottom of a stream and eat plants or small animal life. When they are full grown, from one to three years old, they crawl out on land and molt their skins to become winged adults.

The large stonefly grows to 2 inches long, as does its nymph. In May and June the full-grown nymphs leave the water to change into adults.

Snowflies are small black stoneflies. The dark-colored nymphs grow to ½ inch long. They change into adults from February to early spring.

MAYFLIES

Mayflies have gray, brown, or light-colored slender bodies with two or three long tails. Their front wings are larger than the back ones. Adult mayflies do not eat. They live only a few hours or days, just long enough to mate and lay their eggs. In spring large numbers of them swarm at twilight over water or around electric lights. The females drop their eggs into water or lay them under water. The eggs hatch into nymphs of different sizes and shapes according to the species. They have three, or sometimes two, tails and seven pairs of gills on each side of the body. Each foot has one claw. They live in water from six weeks to three years. Then they crawl out and shed their skins to become winged insects. In this stage they molt once again. Mayflies are the only insects to molt after they have wings.

The large mayflies sometimes swarm in such numbers that, after the flight, piles of dead are found. The nymphs, which grow to 2 inches long, burrow in mud and eat green ooze.

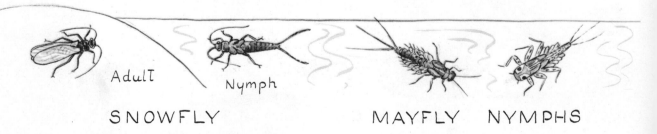

SNOWFLY   MAYFLY NYMPHS

CADDIS FLIES

MOTHS

CADDIS FLIES

Caddis flies are mothlike insects from ⅛ to a little over 1 inch long. They fly at dusk or at night near water or around lights. At rest they fold their brown, gray, or black wings in an upward slope over their backs. They have long legs and long feelers. The females lay eggs under water.

The caddis' worms which hatch from the eggs build cases to live in. These cases are usually tubular, from ½ to 2 inches long. They are held together with a gluey saliva or silk. Some of the materials used in them are tiny pebbles, grains of sand, tiny shells, sticks, seeds, bark, and leaves.

One kind of caddis worm makes a funnel-shaped net in which it catches tiny animal life to eat. Most of the other caddis worms eat leaves of water plants. When they are full grown, they form pupae, usually inside their cases. When ready to change into winged adults, they float or climb up water plants to the surface. As adults, they live only a short time.

MOTHS

A few kinds of moths come from caterpillars which live in water. Two kinds of caterpillars live on water-lily pads in cases made from bits of the lily pad fastened together with silk. One kind breathes through fringe-like gills along the sides of its body. The other kind has no gills and it breathes a bubble of air caught in its leaf case. Both kinds of caterpillars eat leaves. When full grown, the first kind forms a pupa inside its case and changes into a small moth with gray fore wings and white hind wings. The second kind, which is often found on water plants in greenhouses, turns into a small moth with black or brown wings marked with yellow and white.

Another kind of caterpillar lives on rocks in rapid streams. It makes a silken covering which it attaches to a rock. It eats the green ooze on the rock and breathes through two rows of threadlike gills on each side of its body. In June or July it forms a pupa and changes into a moth with gray-brown fore wings and white hind wings with black markings.

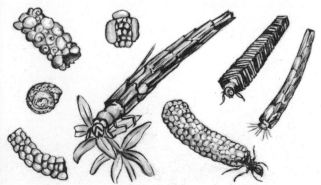

CADDIS WORMS and CASES

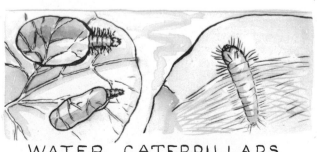

WATER CATERPILLARS

BROWN-PATCH DRAGONFLY

DRAGONFLIES

Many different kinds of dragonflies, from very large to rather small, fly around ponds.

Dragonflies are helpful because they eat mosquitoes, midges, and other small insects. They catch the insects in a trap made by curling their feet under their bodies while flying.

Female dragonflies drop their eggs into water or lay them in the stems or leaves of water plants. The eggs hatch into hard-skinned nymphs. The nymphs crawl about the bottom of the pond for a year or more and grow to be ½ to 1½ inches long. They eat small water life which they capture by thrusting out their long underjaws. They breathe by taking water in and out of their tails and they shoot forward by squirting out the water.

When the nymphs are ready to change into adults they climb up stems into the air. Their skin splits down the back and a dragonfly with crumpled wings emerges. The wings soon spread out.

The brown-patch dragonfly has a brown and black body. Its wingspread is 3¾ inches and the lower wings have a large brown patch. The nymph is green and brown and 1 inch long.

The green-and-brown dragonfly has clear wings with a spread of 2½ inches and a green, brown, and black body. The brown nymph is ⅝ inch long.

Amberwings have short bodies and a wingspread of about 1½ inches. The females have amber blotches on the wings and the males are all amber.

The red dragonflies have a wingspread of about 2 inches. They fly over ponds and fields in autumn.

Female and young male whitetails have brown bodies with yellow spots on the sides. Old males have a white abdomen. The wingspread is 2⅝ inches.

The ten-spot is one of a large family of dragonflies. Each one has a different number of brown spots on the wings. Its wingspread is 3¾ inches.

The large green darner is found the world over. Its body is green and its wingspread over 4 inches.

Even larger is the giant dragonfly. It is often seen around houses, especially in fall.

GREEN-and-BROWN DRAGONFLY

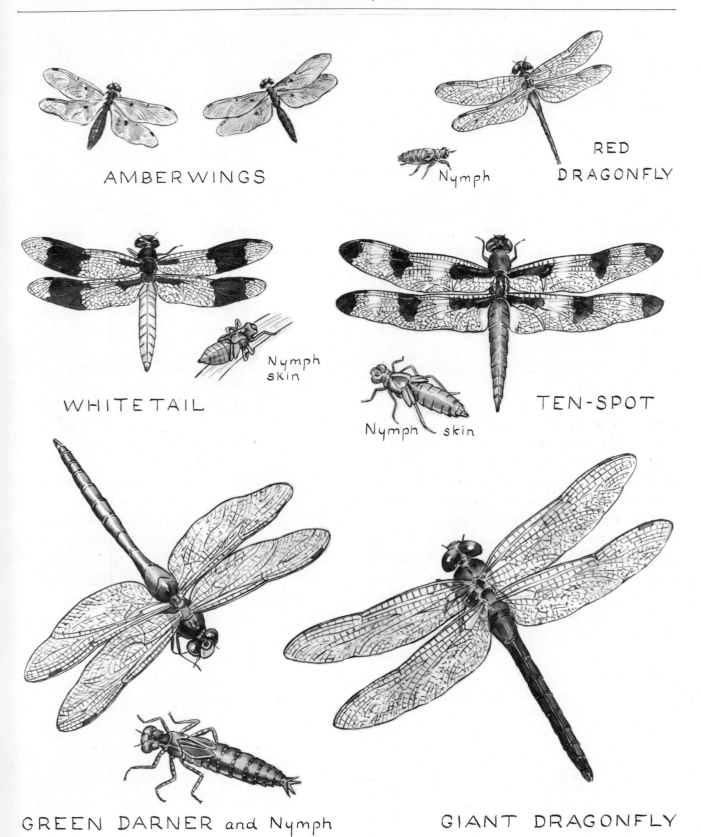

AMBERWINGS

Nymph

RED
DRAGONFLY

WHITETAIL

Nymph
skin

Nymph skin

TEN-SPOT

GREEN DARNER and Nymph

GIANT DRAGONFLY

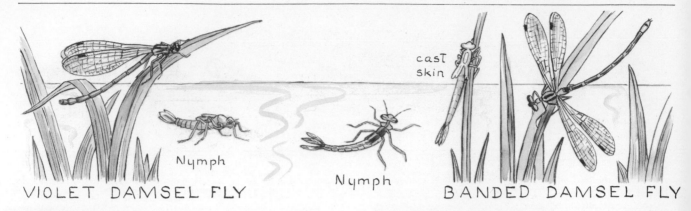

VIOLET DAMSEL FLY

BANDED DAMSEL FLY

DAMSEL FLIES

Damsel flies are smaller than most dragonflies and more slender. They fold their wings over their backs when they rest. Usually they fly more slowly than dragonflies. Sometimes the male and female fly together, the male clasping the female around her neck with his tail end. He sometimes assists her when she lays eggs by going into the water with her or by pulling her out afterward. The eggs are usually laid in the leaves of water plants.

Small nymphs hatch from the eggs. They often stay on the plants, where they catch mosquito wrigglers and other small insects to eat. At their tail ends the nymphs have three flat gills through which they breathe. The nymphs live in the water through the winter. In spring and summer the nymph crawls out on land to change into an adult. It splits its skin down the back and the newly-formed damsel fly emerges.

The violet damsel fly has a violet-colored body,

the male being brighter. The female lays her eggs on floating mats of algae in shallow water, the male holding onto her during the process. The nymph is about ½ inch long.

The banded damsel fly has a brown or black body with green or blue bands. The delicate, almost transparent nymph is bright green with brown markings and is about ⅝ of an inch long.

Ruby-spot damsel flies are seen late in summer. The males have a bright red spot at the base of the wings and the females a light red spot. The brown or green nymphs, which grow to 1¼ inches long, live in moving water.

The handsome black-wing damsel flies have metallic blue or green bodies. Their black wings are a little wider than those of most damsel flies. The female has a white spot near the tip of each wing. She lays her eggs in the stems of plants just below the surface of the water. The nymphs grow to 1 inch long.

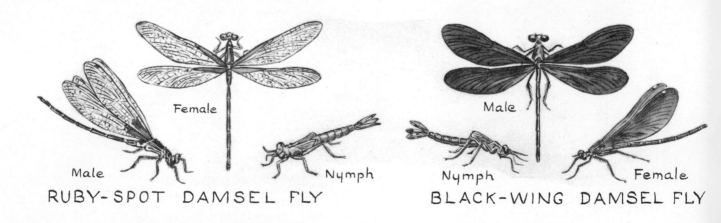

RUBY-SPOT DAMSEL FLY

BLACK-WING DAMSEL FLY

CRAWLING WATER BEETLES

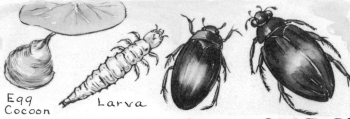

WATER SCAVENGER BEETLES

BEETLES

Water beetles go through four stages: the egg, the larva or grub, the pupa, and the adult insect.

The crawling water beetle is a very small one (less than ¼ inch long) which crawls among water plants and eats pond scum. It is brown with yellow marks. It breathes under water from an air bubble stored in its body. The female lays eggs in spring and summer on water plants. The larvae are small and slender; some kinds have threadlike gills along the sides. They eat scum. When full grown, they form pupae in moist earth.

Whirligig beetles are black or dark brown. Some kinds are ¼ inch long; others, ½ inch. Numbers of them often whirl about on the surface of still water. When under water they carry a bubble of air under their wings. If annoyed they squeak and give off an odor. The females lay eggs under lily pads and other water plants. The larvae (½ and 1 inch long) are pale and slender with a row of fringed gills on each side. The larvae eat small water insects. When full grown, they crawl out on moist earth and form pupae inside cocoons.

Water scavenger beetles are black and from ½ to 1½ inches long. They eat water plants, small animal life, and decaying matter. When under water they breathe a film of air carried on the underside of the body. The females lay their eggs enclosed in a waterproof cocoon, usually attached to a water plant. The larvae are rather stout and ½ inch or more in length. They eat water insects and decaying plants. In late summer they form pupae in earth. The adult beetles can fly and are sometimes seen around lights.

The several kinds of diving beetles vary in length from less than ½ inch to over 2 inches. They are black, sometimes marked with yellow. They often hang head down in the water with the tail end sticking up for air. Before diving, they collect an air bubble under their wings.

In spring the females lay eggs on or in water plants. The larvae (some kinds 3 inches long) are called water tigers because of the fierce way they go after their prey. They eat water insects, and the larger ones attack tadpoles and small fish. They breathe by sticking their tail end up to the surface. When they are a month or more old, they form pupae in moist earth.

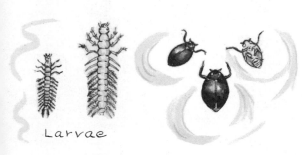

WHIRLIGIG BEETLES

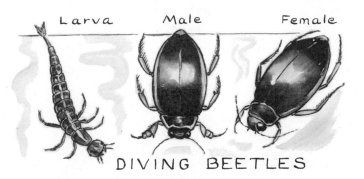

DIVING BEETLES

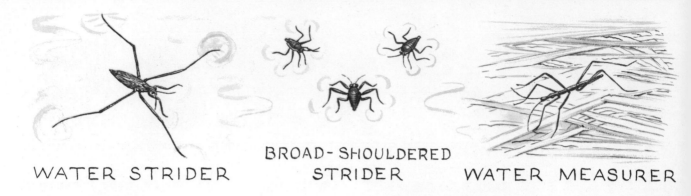

WATER STRIDER   BROAD-SHOULDERED
                         STRIDER   WATER MEASURER

WATER BUGS

Water striders are long-legged bugs which skim over the water. Their feet make dimples in its surface but do not sink in. The striders travel on their two back pairs of legs and grasp their food in the front pair. They eat insects which come up from under water or fall from branches above. Sometimes a strider plunges under water carrying a film of air around its body. The females lay their eggs at the surface on plants or other support. The eggs hatch in about two weeks into young which look and act like the adults.

The large water striders are about ½ inch long in the body and have legs that are much longer. Some kinds do not have wings.

The broad-shouldered water strider is only ⅛ inch long in the body. It sometimes swims upside down under the surface film.

The water measurer is a slender bug which walks on mats of water weeds. It is hard to see, as its ½-inch-long body looks so much like a stem. It seems to measure each step as it walks slowly on its long thin legs. It eats small water insects and other tiny creatures. The females lay eggs in spring and early summer on stems above the water.

The slender water scorpion is another sticklike bug. Its body is brown and grows to over 2 inches long. It lives under water, often near the surface, with the long tube at the end of its body sticking up for air. With its four long, thin back legs it climbs over water plants. Its two front legs, like slender claws, are used to grasp its prey—small creatures such as damsel-fly and mayfly nymphs. The females lay eggs on underwater plants. In two or three weeks the eggs hatch into small wingless scorpions.

The broad water scorpion is about ½ inch long, not counting the air tube at the end of its body. It crawls about the plants and dead leaves at the edge of a pond, looking for small creatures to eat. Grasping its prey in its front legs, it sucks out the juices. The females lay their eggs in the decayed tissue of plants. The eggs hatch into small insects shaped like the parents.

(SLENDER)   WATER SCORPIONS   (BROAD)

The giant and smaller water bugs have flat bodies and clawlike front legs. The giant bug, which is also called the electric-light bug, sometimes flies around lights. One kind grows to 1½ inches long and some kinds are larger. In the water this bug crawls along the muddy bottom, looking for dragonfly nymphs, small fish, and other creatures to eat. With its strong beak it can bite hard. Be careful if you catch one! The females lay their eggs on rubbish or weeds in the water. In a week or two the eggs hatch into young which are like the adults except that they are small and have no wings.

The smaller water bug grows to about 1 inch long. Its habits are like those of the larger kind except for its peculiar way of laying eggs. The female fastens her eggs to the back of the male and he has to carry them around for a week or more until they hatch.

Water boatmen are small oblong bugs, ¼ inch or longer, with fine dark lines on their wings. They paddle themselves right side up through the water, using their hind legs as oars. With their front legs they anchor themselves to an underwater support. They also use their front legs to scrape up the ooze and other plant stuff which they eat.

Although boatmen are not able to breathe under the water, they stay in it most of the time, coming to the surface often for air. At night they sometimes fly around lights. The females lay their yellow eggs on trash under water. The young are

WATER BOATMEN

BACK-SWIMMERS

light colored and without wings. The adults remain active through the winter.

Backswimmers are about ½ inch long and are usually light colored on the back and dark underneath. This is because they swim upside down with their underside on top. They use their hind legs for oars. They often come to the surface and sometimes hang head down with their tail end sticking out. When they dive below, they carry a film of air on the hairs of their underside. The females lay their eggs in or on underwater plant stems.

Backswimmers eat tiny water creatures which they catch in their front legs or paralyze by stinging with their beaks. They can sting people also.

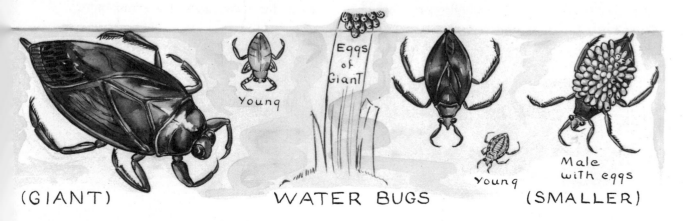

(GIANT) WATER BUGS (SMALLER)

BROOK LAMPREY

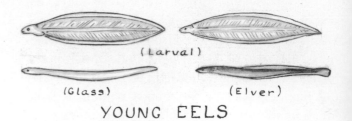

(Larval)

(Glass)   (Elver)

YOUNG EELS

LAMPREYS

In spring and early summer lampreys run upstream to spawn. The male, often helped by the female, makes a nest on the stony bottom by pushing or carrying the stones aside to make a hollow place. The female then lays her thousands of tiny eggs in the nest. She fans a layer of sand over them with her tail fin and leaves them.

The young, which hatch in one to three weeks, are small, blind, and wormlike. They burrow into mud and feed on tiny organisms. It is four or five years before they are ready to become adult lampreys and enter lakes. As adults, they will live a year or two and die after spawning.

The lake lamprey is a snakelike creature, more primitive than a fish. Originally a salt-water dweller, it now lives in the Great Lakes and other northern lakes. There it grows to 15 inches or longer. It is bluish-gray, sometimes mottled with brown. For a mouth it has a suction disk lined with horny teeth. With this disk it fastens itself to the side of a fish. After making a hole in the fish's side with its teeth and tongue, it proceeds to suck the blood which is its food.

The brook lamprey is a small variety which spends all its life in a brook or river. It does not fasten onto fish. The young eat small water life.

EELS

Eels are long, snakelike fish. They have a pair of fins behind the head and a long fin that extends along the back, around the tail, and under the body. They are greenish- or yellowish-brown, or black on the back and lighter underneath. Females grow to 3 feet or longer and males to about 2 feet.

Eels live in fresh water, in the eastern states, for about eight years; then they go downstream to the Atlantic Ocean to spawn. At this time they are dark on the back, silvery on the sides, and are called silver eels. They travel through the Atlantic to the Sargasso Sea, southeast of Bermuda. There, deep in the ocean, each female lays millions of tiny eggs. The eggs hatch into flat, transparent, leaf-shaped creatures which live in the sea for a year and grow to about 3 inches in length.

Gradually these larval eels work their way to the surface of the ocean near the coast of America. By now they are rounded, but still small and transparent, and are called glass eels. In spring these young eels, or elvers, start up streams, traveling mostly at night. They become darker and develop fins. The females go far upstream, while the males stay in the lower part of the stream.

Eels eat many kinds of water creatures and plants.

LAKE LAMPREY

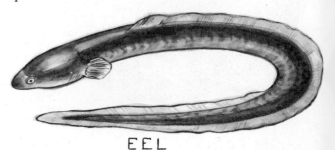

EEL

ALEWIFE

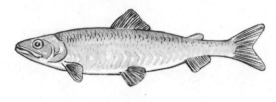

SMELT

HERRING

The alewife and the shad belong to the herring family. Each has one fin in the middle of the back and a forked tail. In autumn and winter they live in the Atlantic Ocean. In spring they run up rivers and streams to spawn. That is when they are usually caught by fishermen.

The alewife, or big-eyed herring, usually enters fresh water in March or April, two or three weeks before the shad. It is bluish or greenish on the back, silvery on the sides, and it grows to about 15 inches long. Because of the sharp scales on its underside it is also called a sawbelly.

The female alewife lays about 100,000 eggs, which hatch in a week or less. By autumn the young are about 4 inches long. Then they and the adult fish swim out to sea.

Shad are silvery like the alewife, but are much larger, sometimes reaching a length of 2½ feet. In spring the males go up the streams first. The females follow and each one lays from 30,000 to 150,000 eggs. The eggs hatch in from six to ten days, depending on the temperature of the water. The adult fish return to the sea when the water in the stream becomes warm. The young fish swim out to sea in summer when they are 3 to 5 inches in length.

SMELT AND SALMON

Smelts are small fish which live in the Atlantic and Pacific oceans and some eastern lakes. In late winter or early spring the smelts that live in the sea run up the streams to spawn. One female may lay 50,000 eggs before she returns to the sea.

In shape and arrangement of fins the smelt and salmon resemble each other. In color the smelt is greenish on the back and silvery on the sides. Although it usually does not grow to more than 8 inches long, it is an important food fish. Smelts are caught with nets and with hook and line.

The Atlantic salmon lives in the ocean and swims upriver in winter and spring to spawn. It is no longer plentiful all along the coast but it is still found in northern rivers. Some salmon live in lakes and do not swim to the sea at all. In spring they follow the smelts upstream.

The female salmon makes a nest in the gravel bed of the stream and lays from 200 to 21,000 eggs. The eggs hatch in about three weeks. The young fish live in the stream until their second or third spring. Then they swim down to the sea. Salmon are dark on the back and silvery on the sides, with black and red spots. In the sea salmon weigh 25 pounds or more. In lakes they weigh about 10 pounds.

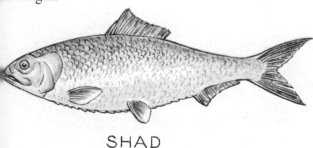

SHAD

ATLANTIC SALMON

BROOK TROUT

BROWN TROUT

TROUT

Trout are of the same family as salmon. They are fine food fish of medium or small size. Usually they live in fresh water, but some, like the rainbow trout, live part of the time in salt water. There are different kinds of trout in different parts of the country. Their colors change with the kind of water in which they live, so it is not always easy to identify them.

One of the best-known trout is the brook trout. It lives in most of the United States in swift-flowing, cool streams, especially those with deep pools and overhanging banks. In small brooks it grows to only 6 or 8 inches long, but in larger streams it may reach 18 inches and weigh several pounds. In color the brook trout is olive, mottled with dark brown or black on the back and spotted with red on the sides. The lower fins are white, orange, and black.

When the water grows cool in the fall, brook trout go up small creeks to shallow places with a gravel bottom in order to spawn. The males go first and the females follow. The females make nests in the gravel and lay from several hundred to several thousand eggs. When the water begins to get warm the following spring, the eggs hatch.

Lake trout live in northern lakes. They sometimes go into shallow water to feed and, in the fall, to spawn. The young hatch in late winter or early spring. In color the lake trout is usually dark with light spots on the sides. It weighs 9 pounds or less on an average, but may be much heavier. These trout were plentiful in the Great Lakes, but commercial fishing has greatly reduced their numbers.

Brown trout, which were introduced from Europe some time ago, are now found in streams all over this country. They are dark brown with black and red spots on the back and sides and lighter underneath. The brown trout may weigh 7 pounds or more. It feeds mostly at night either at the surface or on the bottom. In the fall it swims upstream to spawn in shallow water.

The rainbow trout is a Pacific Coast fish which has been introduced into eastern streams where it is able to live in warm, quiet water. Sometimes it swims out to sea, returning to the stream at spawning time in late winter or early spring. In fresh water it usually has a broad pink band along the sides and dark spots on the upper side and tail. In the sea it is silvery and the spots disappear. It grows to 18 inches and longer and weighs from 2 to 8 or more pounds.

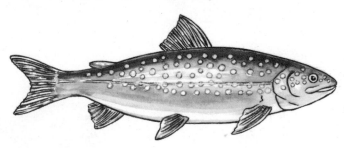

LAKE TROUT

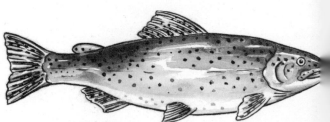

RAINBOW TROUT

YELLOW PERCH

WHITE PERCH

PERCH AND PIKE

Yellow perch are caught by fishermen in lakes, ponds, and streams all over the country. They are from 10 to 14 inches long and weigh a pound or more. In color they are olive on the back, yellow with dark bars on the sides, and white underneath. The lower fins are orange or red, being brighter in spring at spawning time. The females lay their eggs in long strings of jelly among water weeds.

The pike perch, or walleyed pike, belongs to the perch family. It lives in large, clear streams or lakes in most of the East and Middle West. Usually it weighs from 3 to 4 pounds, sometimes more. In color it is brown and yellow. Its milky eyes give it the name walleyed. In spawns in April or May, and the eggs hatch in from fourteen to thirty days.

The white perch, which really belongs to the bass family, is often caught in streams in the eastern states. It lives in both fresh and salt water and grows to a length of 15 inches and a weight of from 2 to 3 pounds. On the back it is olive; the sides are silvery without any dark bars. The females lay eggs in May and June and the young hatch in about a week.

Pickerel are small pike which live in slow streams and ponds in most of the eastern states. They feed on minnows and other water creatures which they catch while hiding under floating leaves. Their mottled olive-green and golden-brown coloring makes them hard to see. Pickerel grow to 2 feet long and several pounds in weight. In early spring they spawn in shallow, weedy water. The eggs hatch in about two weeks.

The large pike which lives in lakes and streams in the northern states grows to 4 feet long and 40 pounds in weight, though the average is 5 pounds. It is bluish or greenish with long, light spots on the sides and light underneath. It spawns in winter and early spring, and the eggs hatch in from two to four weeks.

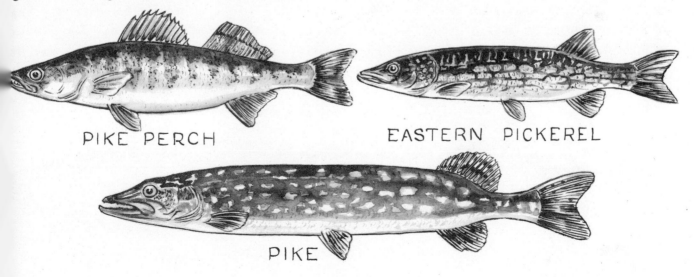

PIKE PERCH

EASTERN PICKEREL

PIKE

BULLHEAD (HORNED POUT)

CATFISH

Catfish are heavy bodied, flat headed and smooth skinned. They have barbels, like whiskers, around their large mouths. There are a number of different kinds in this country.

The common bullhead, or horned pout, is a small catfish which is found in ponds and sluggish streams in the eastern states. It is dark gray or brownish, sometimes with yellowish markings. It grows about a foot long and may weigh from 3 to 4 pounds, though usually less. It is caught with almost any kind of bait and is fairly good eating.

In late spring the male bullhead clears a round place in the gravel at the bottom of the pond and the female lays her eggs in it. The male guards the eggs and the young which soon hatch from them. In early summer you may see schools of small coal-black bullheads. The small bullheads may be raised in an aquarium on bits of raw meat, fish, worms, algae, and ground dog biscuit. Full-grown bullheads eat small water creatures, which they catch by feeling in the mud with their whiskers.

The yellow bullhead is about the same size as the horned pout. It can be identified by the bright yellow on its underside. The black bullhead is darker and smaller, growing to 6 inches or more.

Stonecats, or mad toms, are small catfish from 3 to 6 inches long. They are common in the Middle West, where they live in the shallow parts of rapid streams, hiding under stones or plants. They have poison glands at the base of their forward (pectoral) and back (dorsal) fins. In June and July they lay masses of yellow eggs, attaching them to the underside of stones.

Very large catfish live in lakes and rivers. The blue catfish weighs up to 20 pounds. The channel catfish, gray spotted with black, weighs from 5 to 25 pounds.

STONECAT   CHANNEL CATFISH

THREE-SPINED STICKLEBACK

STICKLEBACKS

These small fish live in streams and shallow ponds in the eastern and other parts of the country. You can tell different kinds apart by the number of spines on their backs.

The three-spined stickleback grows to 3 or 4 inches long and is common in brooks, ponds, and sometimes salt marshes. It is greenish on the sides, with dark bars; the male is orange underneath. The male makes a nest from rootlets and stalks of water plants. The nest is shaped like an igloo and is held together by a sticky secretion from special glands in the fish's body. Several females lay their eggs in one nest. After they leave, the male fertilizes and guards the eggs.

The brook stickleback has five spines on its back. The male grows to 2 inches and the female to ½ inch longer. At breeding time, in spring, the male is black on the back and yellowish underneath; the female is olive with darker blotches.

The male makes a nest from pieces of water-plant stems, fibers, and algae, which he bites off and cements together with mucus. The nest is hollow through the center and is about the size and shape of a walnut. It is usually attached to an underwater stem. One female, or more, lays her eggs in the nest. The male guards the eggs for the ten days or so that it takes them to hatch.

These fish are ready to breed when they are a year old; they usually do not live more than six months after that. A pair of brook sticklebacks makes interesting aquarium pets. Put them in a large tank with plenty of water plants. Do not include other fish. Give them an upright stick to build on and they will probably make a nest and lay eggs. The young fish will eat finely ground fish food, water fleas, and other tiny water life. The adults eat fish food, small worms, and insects.

The ten-spined stickleback lives in cool water and grows to about 3 inches long.

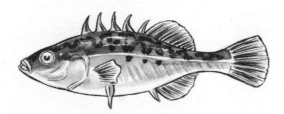

BROOK STICKLEBACK

TEN-SPINED STICKLEBACK

PUMPKINSEED

SUNFISH

Sunfish are short, flat fish which are found in ponds all over the country. Different kinds live in different places, and all are good to eat.

The pumpkinseed is the common sunfish found from Maine to Florida. It grows to 8 inches long and is shaped like its name. It is dark on the back, iridescent blue-and-green with olive bars and orange flecks on the sides, and orange underneath. The ear flaps are black with a red spot. The male is more brightly colored than the female.

In May or June the male makes a nest on the pond bottom by clearing out a circular space. He drives a female to the nest, where she lays her eggs. The eggs stick to the small stones in the nest, and the female swims away, leaving the male to guard them. In warm water the eggs hatch in less than a week. After a few days in the nest the young swim out and are able to care for themselves.

Young pumpkinseeds and other sunfish are pretty in an aquarium. They will eat small worms, insects, and bits of meat.

The bluegill, or red-breasted sunfish, lives in lakes and quiet streams all over the country. Formerly found in the East, it has now been introduced into the western states. It grows to 12 inches or more in length, about 1 pound in weight, and is good eating. In color it is greenish-olive on the back and reddish-orange underneath; the ear flaps are dark blue or black.

The long-eared sunfish is colored much like the bluegill, but it has longer ear flaps with bright-colored lower edges and a larger mouth. In the North it grows to 8 inches and weighs 1 pound. In the South, where it is more common, it grows larger.

BLUEGILL

LONG-EARED SUNFISH

ROCK BASS

CALICO BASS

BASS

Bass belong to the same family as sunfish and have the same arrangement of fins.

The rock bass, or rock sunfish, is olive-green with dark markings. It grows to 12 inches and weighs 1 pound or more. It lives in clear, cool lakes and streams in the central part of the country. In late spring or early summer the male makes and defends a nest the same way the sunfish does.

The calico bass, or black crappie, and the white crappie are found in ponds all over the country. Both are so good to eat that they are often "planted" in farm fish ponds. Both kinds grow to about 1 foot in length and are silvery-olive with dark green markings; the calico bass has more of the dark markings. In early summer they make gravel nests, usually in deep water.

Small-mouthed and large-mouthed black bass are popular game fish in all parts of the country. Both may be found in the same water, often where their favorite food, crayfish, is plentiful. Usually the small-mouthed bass likes clear, cool water; the large-mouthed bass, warmer water.

In May or June the males make nests, like small basins, in shallow places on the pond bottom. Each male persuades one or more females to enter the nest and lay her eggs. The eggs are glued together in strings and stick to stones in the nest. They hatch in a week or two and the young stay in the nest about ten days. The male guards the eggs and the young.

Black bass are a mottled greenish-brown rather than black; the color varies from light to dark in different localities. The small-mouthed bass grows to from 1 to 2 feet and weighs from 2 to 5 pounds or more. The large-mouthed bass grows to over 2 feet in the South; seldom to more than 8 inches and a weight of 2 or 3 pounds in the North. You can tell one fish from the other by the mouth. It extends beyond the eye in the large-mouthed bass, and to a line just below the eye in the small-mouthed bass.

SMALL-MOUTHED

LARGE-MOUTHED

BLACK BASS

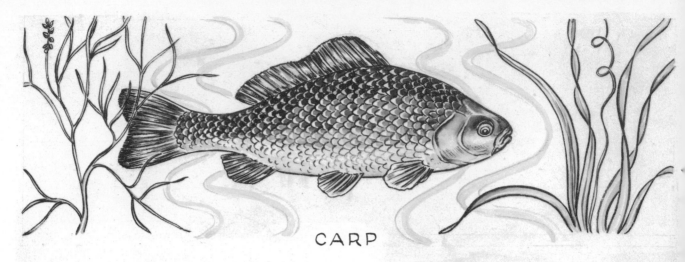

CARP

CARP

About eighty years ago a few hundred carp were brought to this country from Europe. They were put into breeding ponds where they increased so fast that it was soon possible to distribute them around the country. Now they are common everywhere.

The carp is a fairly good food fish, though it sometimes has a muddy taste. It grows to 2 feet or more and to 16 or more pounds. In color it varies from dark greenish-brown or blackish to golden-red or silvery. It has coarse scales, one long fin on the back and two small feelers on each side of the face. It feeds on the muddy bottom, on water plants and small animal life.

In May and June carp lay their eggs in shallow water. One female may lay nearly two million eggs, so it is easy to see how these fish have increased and spread all around the world.

Goldfish are members of the carp family. Originally they lived in Asia. Fish breeders in China, Korea, and Japan have bred a number of different kinds of fancy goldfish, such as the comet. In this country many of them are raised in aquariums.

Aquarium goldfish are either golden or silvery, or black and white. Many of them will live in outdoor pools as well as in aquariums. In ponds that do not freeze solid they will live through the winter and grow as long as 18 inches. They sometimes increase so fast as to become a nuisance.

In spring a female goldfish, two or more years old, lays from ten to twenty eggs at one time on water plants. The eggs stick to the plants; in warm water they hatch in a week or less. The young goldfish are dull in color, becoming brightly colored when they are several months old. Goldfish that live in ponds for several generations lose their bright colors.

COMMON

COMET

GOLDFISH

FALLFISH

GOLDEN SHINER

Some kinds of fish which belong to the carp family are native to this country. Some of them are large enough for food; others are minnows which are used for bait.

The fallfish, or chub, lives in swift streams and clear lakes in the eastern states. It grows to 1 foot or more and weighs up to 3 pounds. It has large scales and a rather large mouth. On the back it is steel-blue; on the sides and underneath, silvery. In spring the males are rosy underneath. Fallfish eat insects, small fish, and algae.

The horned dace, or creek chub, lives in brooks and weedy ponds in most of the eastern part of the country. It grows to about 10 inches. On the back it is grayish-blue; underneath it is whitish, or rosy on males in spring. Then the males have orange heads covered with small tubercles.

In spring the male makes a nest in a gravel ridge on the pond bottom. The nest is a shallow hole with a wall of stones around it. One or more females enter the nest and lay eggs which the male guards.

The golden shiner lives in shallow ponds in the eastern and southern states. It grows to 1 foot in length and 1 pound or more in weight. On the back it is greenish-gold; on the sides, silvery; the fins are yellow. At breeding time the body is yellow. The females lay eggs on water plants or rubbish. Golden shiners are often raised for bait.

The common shiner, or redfin, lives in brooks and creeks over most of the country. Its length varies from 5 to 8 inches. On the back it is olive-green; on the sides, silvery-white. In spring the males are iridescent blue on the back, pinkish on the sides. They have red borders on the fins and small horny growths on the head.

In May and June the males make the nests, basin-shaped clearings in the gravel bottom of streams. Sometimes they use the nests of other fish. One or more females lay orange-colored eggs in the nest. The male guards the eggs but not the young. Common shiners are used for bait, especially for black bass. Small shiners are attractive in aquariums.

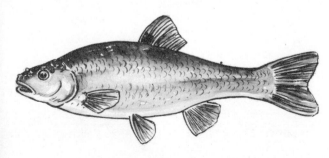

HORNED DACE

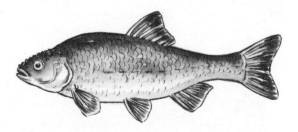

COMMON SHINER

MINNOWS and other small fishes

BLACK-NOSED DACE

Length: to 3 inches. Color: olive-green on back, light silvery on sides, black stripe from nose to tail; in spring male has orange on fins. Home: brooks in eastern part of the United States; will live in aquariums also.

MUD MINNOW or ROCKFISH

Length: 4 to 5 inches. Color: dark green or brownish with light stripes along sides. Home: the bottom of streams, ponds, and swamps along the eastern coast. Mud minnows sometimes bury themselves in the mud.

BLUNT-NOSED MINNOW

Length: to 4 inches. Color: olive on back, bluish and silvery on sides. Home: small streams in eastern United States. In late spring the female glues her eggs to the underside of stones and the male guards them.

FRESH-WATER KILLIFISH

Length: 2½ to 4 inches. Color: olive-green or brown on back; silvery with dark bars on sides. Home: lakes and marshy streams. Different kinds live in different parts of the country. Killifish make good aquarium and small-pool fish.

CUTLIPS MINNOW

The underjaw is divided into three parts. Length: to 8 inches. Color: dark, almost black on male at breeding time in late spring. Home: slow streams in the eastern states. The female lays yellow eggs in a stone nest made and guarded by the male.

BROOK SILVERSIDES

Length: 3 to 4 inches. Color: translucent light olive-green, silver stripe on side. These small fish swim in schools near surface along shores of lakes and streams in central and southern states. They are attractive in an aquarium.

JOHNNY DARTER   SCULPIN   STONE ROLLER

BOTTOM FEEDERS

The Johnny darter is a small perch which grows to 3 inches or less. It is olive-brown with black markings on the back and fins. It lives at the bottom of a brook where it rests on its front fins, climbs among water weeds, or darts after its food. It can turn both its head and its bulging eyes. In May and June the females lay eggs, attaching them to the underside of stones.

The sculpin, or miller's-thumb, lives in rocky brooks and lakes. It is a small fish, from 5 to 6 inches long, with oversized head and fins. Its olive-brown body speckled with dark brown blends with the muddy bottom. It feeds on small water creatures, algae, and some fish eggs. In spring the female lays orange-colored eggs in clusters on the underside of stones in shallow water. The male guards the eggs.

The stone roller lives in shallow streams where it feeds on vegetable matter which it sucks up with mud from the bottom. It grows to about 8 inches in length. On the back it is dark with a coppery sheen. In spring the male has orange or red fins, and small tubercles on the head and body. He makes a hollow nest in the sand or gravel in which the female lays her eggs.

The two large suckers pictured below feed on the muddy bottom of ponds and streams. Their mouths are on the underside of their heads and their lips stick out to suck in mud with the small animal life that may be in it.

The common white sucker grows to 12 inches or less in small streams, but in rivers and lakes it may reach 18 inches or more. On the back it is light or dark olive; lighter underneath. At spawning time, around May or June, the male's fins are tinged with red. At this time the suckers swim upstream and the females lay their eggs in shallow water. Two males mate with one female. After hatching, the young fish swim near the surface for about ten days. They do not have sucking mouths at first.

The redhorse sucker, which lives in swift streams and lakes in Canada and the northern states, grows to 2 feet in length and 8 pounds in weight. It is yellowish or olive on the back and lighter underneath. The tail and lower fins are red and brighter in spring when the fish swim upstream to spawn.

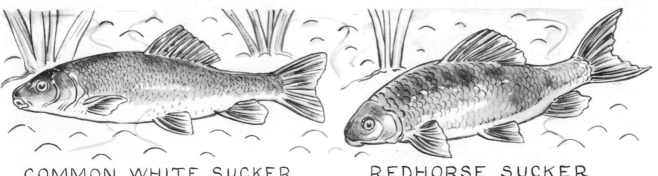

COMMON WHITE SUCKER   REDHORSE SUCKER

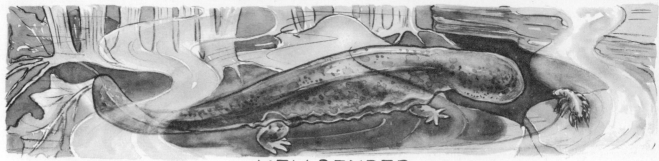

HELLBENDER

LARGE SALAMANDERS

Salamanders live in the water and along the banks of streams as well as in the woods. Most of them are from 4 to 8 inches long, but the two shown on this page are much larger.

The hellbender, which grows to 18 or more inches long, is one of the largest salamanders. It lives in creeks, rivers, and lakes in the eastern part of the country. Usually it stays on the bottom among rocks and rubbish. Its reddish-brown coloring blends so well with the background that it is not often seen. It has a broad, flat head and a flattened body with a wrinkled fold of loose skin along the sides. At night it feeds on crayfish and other small water animals which crawl along the bottom. Although it has lungs, the hellbender usually breathes through its skin.

In autumn the male hellbender makes a nest by clearing a hollow place under a rock in the bed of the stream. The female lays tangled strings of eggs in the nest. The male guards the eggs for two weeks or more until they hatch. The larvae which hatch from the eggs have external gills. The gills remain until the second year, when the larvae are about 4 or 5 inches long. At three or four years they are mature and about 12 inches long.

The mud puppy is another large salamander. It gets its name from the doglike head with wavy red gills which look a little like ears. The body is mottled brown with black spots. It is slimy and about 12 inches long.

Mud puppies live in rivers, quiet streams, and lakes which have water weeds. They are found chiefly in the eastern states. They crawl along the bottom at night, looking for water insects, snails, fish eggs, small fish, and other creatures to eat. They are active through most of the year.

Mud puppies mate in autumn, but the female does not lay her eggs until late spring. She glues the jelly-coated eggs to the underpart of logs or stones. Then she guards them until hatching time, from six to nine weeks later. The newly hatched larvae are about ¾ inch long. It takes seven or eight years for them to become mature. Then they are about 8 inches long. They may live more than twenty years.

MUD PUPPY

SPOTTED SALAMANDER Eggs

AXOLOTL
TIGER SALAMANDER

MOLE SALAMANDERS

These stout-bodied, broad-headed salamanders live on moist land most of the time. They feed on insects, snails, worms, and other small creatures. At breeding time they take to the water. The newly hatched larvae look like tadpoles with external gills.

Spotted salamanders are black with yellow spots. They grow to 7 inches in length. They become slimy when annoyed. In spring the females lay their eggs in shallow pools. The eggs, larger than a frog's, are in jelly-covered masses several inches across. After a few weeks they hatch into greenish-brown larvae, ½ inch long. The larvae live in the water until the end of summer. Then they are about 3 inches long and ready to develop lungs. They go to live in moist woods or meadows; sometimes they get into cellars. Spotted salamanders have been known to live twenty-four years.

The marbled salamander is black and white and grows to 5 inches long. It lives in sandy and rocky places. In autumn it goes to ponds to breed. The females lay their clusters of eggs under some shelter near the shore. The eggs do not hatch until spring, when they are moistened by rains or rising water. The larvae are ¾ inch long. They wriggle to the water if it does not cover them and live in it until the end of summer.

Tiger salamanders are black with yellow blotches. Females average 7 inches; males, 8 inches long. Early in spring the females lay jelly-coated egg masses attached to something under water. In three or four weeks the eggs hatch into greenish ½-inch larvae which live in the water until the end of summer. In some parts of western United States this salamander remains a water creature all its life and is called an axolotl.

Jefferson's salamander grows to 7 inches long and is dark brown with small blue spots on the sides. It lives in woods, where it hides under stones and feeds at night. Early in spring it goes to shallow water. There the female lays her eggs in a jelly mass attached to some support. In a month or so the eggs hatch into ½-inch larvae. By the end of summer the larvae are about 2 inches long and are ready to leave the water.

MARBLED SALAMANDERS

JEFFERSON'S SALAMANDER

DUSKY SALAMANDERS

RED SALAMANDER

LUNGLESS SALAMANDERS

These medium-sized, slender salamanders live among rocks at the edge of streams and in other wet places. They breathe through the throat membrane and the skin, which must be kept moist. The larvae usually have external gills and live in water.

The dusky salamander is reddish- or grayish-brown with dark spots on the back and sides. An old one may be all dark brown. There is a light line from the eye to the mouth. In summer the female lays from twelve to twenty-six jelly-coated eggs in bunches like grapes in moist places under moss, leaves, stones, or other covering. She usually stays with the eggs until they hatch in about two months. The larvae are brown with a row of light spots on each side of the back. They live on land for the first two weeks or so, until their gills and tail fin develop and they are about ¾ inch long. Then they enter water and stay there until the following spring, when they lose their gills and are about 1 inch long. After two years they are 2 inches long and mature. Full-grown males are 5½ inches long;

females are smaller. Dusky salamanders hunt mostly at night for insects, worms, and snails.

The red salamander lives in or near streams and springs in the eastern states, but not in New England. The young salamanders are bright red with black spots on the back and light underneath. The older ones are purplish-brown and are from 4 to 5 inches long. In autumn the female lays her eggs, fifty or more in bunches of ten to twenty-four. She fastens them to the underside of a stone in the water. The eggs hatch late in autumn into brownish-colored larvae which do not become active until spring. They live in water until they are two and a half years old and from 3 to 4 inches long. Then they lose their gills and become bright red. They hunt at night for worms and insects.

The purple salamander lives in small cool streams in the woods where it hides under stones and eats small water creatures. It is more often light red or brownish than purple, and it has dark specks on its back. It is rather stout-bodied and grows to 7 inches long.

Eggs   Larva

DUSKY SALAMANDER

PURPLE SALAMANDER

TWO-LINED SALAMANDER

The two-lined salamander is another lungless one which hides among rocks at the edge of a stream. It is grayish-brown, speckled with black, and has a dark line on each side of its back. Underneath it is yellowish. It grows to nearly 4 inches long and is very active. It is not easy to catch, but if you do succeed in getting hold of one, do not grab it by the tail; it breaks off easily.

If you want to keep a two-lined salamander, put it in a container which is securely covered with a fine screen; it is able to squeeze through a very small opening. Captive salamanders will sometimes eat bits of raw meat dangled from a straw.

Two-lined salamanders mate in spring and summer. The female lays eggs under a rock or other support in the water; each egg hangs by a bit of jelly. In about ten weeks the eggs hatch into ½-inch young. After about two years they are 2 inches long and ready to become adults. They lose their gills and are able to crawl about the rocks as well as swim in the water. They eat small water creatures including worms, insects, and snails, which they hunt during the day.

RED EFT

SPOTTED NEWT

The spotted newt is a fairly common salamander in the eastern states and Canada. It lives in ponds and quiet streams during the beginning and end of its life; the time between it spends on land.

The breeding adults live in water. In spring, or sometimes autumn, the females lay jelly-coated eggs, one at a time, on plants or some other underwater support. In three or more weeks, depending on the temperature, the eggs hatch into larvae, each with external gills, buds for front feet, and a tail fin. By autumn they are able to leave the water. The gills are replaced by lungs. Legs and a slender tail form and the greenish coloring changes to bright red with darker red spots on the back. The young newts are now called red efts. They live in the woods for a year or longer, then change into mature newts which live in water. In some places the newt skips the eft stage entirely.

Spotted newts grow to nearly 4 inches long. They are olive-green with red and black spots on the back and yellow underneath. They eat insects, snails, and similar food.

Eggs   Larva
TWO-LINED SALAMANDER

Larva

Adult Male

SPOTTED NEWT

Eggs
AMERICAN TOAD

TOADS

Toads live on land most of the time. But in spring, after they leave their winter shelter under rocks, logs, or earth, they seek the nearest pond. There they mate and lay their eggs.

The common American toad has a warty light or dark brown skin. The female's throat is light; the male's is marked with dark specks and swells out when he sings. In April the males arrive at the ponds and start the humming chorus which is their mating song. Soon after, the females come and lay their eggs in long strings of jelly in the water. From five to twelve days later the eggs hatch into black tadpoles. The tadpoles grow fast. When they are two months old, or less, they change into tiny toads ½ inch long. They hop out onto the ground and start looking for insects and worms to eat. In two or three years they are mature. Males grow to 3½ inches in length; females are larger. Toads are useful in the garden to catch insects.

Fowler's toad is about the same size as the common toad or a little smaller. It is more distinctly marked with dark spots and it has a light line down

FOWLER'S TOAD

the middle of the back. It comes out of hibernation and goes to the pond later than the common toad. The harsh trill or screech which is its mating call is sometimes heard as late as July. Usually the females lay their eggs around June. The eggs are in strings of jelly, often in double rows. The tadpoles which hatch from the eggs change into toads before autumn.

Spadefoot toads have a fairly smooth brownish skin with gray underneath and a white throat. They grow to about 2½ inches long. With their large webbed hind feet they dig burrows in loose soil, where they stay during the day. At night they come out to hunt for insects and worms and other small creatures.

These toads are in or near water during their breeding season, sometime between the end of April and September. The males have a harsh *wank* for their call. The females lay strings of jelly-coated eggs in the water. The tadpoles which hatch from the eggs grow to 1 inch long and change into ½-inch toads at the end of summer.

Eggs
SPADEFOOT TOAD

TREE FROGS

Most of the year tree frogs live on land, but in spring they go to ponds to mate and lay their eggs. The tiny spring peepers are among the first to come out of hibernation and enter ponds and puddles. In March crowds of peepers start the shrill piping which is one of the signs of spring.

Although often heard, peepers are not easily seen. Their coloring, light brown with a dark brown cross on the back, blends with the dead leaves and stems on which they sit. They are small, an inch or less long. Sometimes in the evening, with a flashlight, you may see one. If the male is singing, his throat will be puffed out like a little balloon. It is dark; the female's throat is light.

The female peeper lays her jelly-coated eggs separately on leaves and stems in shallow water. From six to twelve days later tiny tadpoles hatch from the eggs. In about three months the tadpoles are a little over an inch long. Then they lose their tails and change into ½-inch peepers. In three or four years they are mature and ready to breed. In summer and autumn the peepers live in meadows or woods. With the sticky pads on their feet they can climb bushes and trees. They eat insects and worms.

The cricket frog is brown, grayish, or olive-green on the back with dark spots and a green line down the middle; underneath it is creamy white. Like the spring peeper, it is no more than an inch long. It comes out of hibernation early in spring and may be heard in the ponds from April until June. Its call, a clicking sound, resembles a

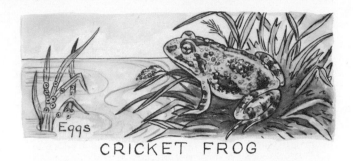

CRICKET FROG

cricket's chirp. The females lay their eggs separately or in small clusters on stems under water.

Although cricket frogs belong to the tree frog family, the pads on their toes are too small for them to climb trees. Most of the time they live along the weedy borders of ponds and swamps. Because they leap so high, they are sometimes called grasshopper frogs.

The tree frog, or toad, is the one we hear singing in trees in summer. It also sings in ponds when it mates in May. Around the first of June the females begin to lay their light brown, jelly-covered eggs in groups on plant stems just under water or floating on the surface. The eggs hatch in four or five days into tadpoles which grow fast. In less than two months the light yellowish, red-tailed tadpoles are usually ready to change into ½-inch frogs.

The tree frog grows to about 2 inches long. It is grayish-green or brownish-gray on the back, with a dark, irregular blotch. Underneath it is light, with orange under the hind legs. The sticky pads on its toes are well developed and it is able to cling to the branches of a tree, sometimes hanging on with one foot.

SPRING PEEPERS

TREE FROGS

WOOD FROG

PICKEREL FROG

WOOD AND MEADOW FROGS

The wood frog lives on the ground among fallen leaves and moss most of the time. Early in spring it enters a pond to mate and lay its eggs. The masses of jelly-coated eggs are usually attached to a support under water. From four days to two weeks later the eggs hatch into tadpoles. The tadpoles eat algae while they grow for two or three months. They have light lines on the upper jaw and are pinkish or bronze underneath. When nearly 2 inches long they change into ½-inch frogs.

Wood frogs grow to 2 or 2½ inches long, the female being the larger. They are light or dark brown, with a black patch behind the eye. They eat insects and other small animal life.

The pickerel frog lives in or near water except sometimes in summer. Then it may hunt for insects and other creatures in the fields. It has dark brown rectangular spots on its light brown back and a light stripe along each side. Underneath it is light with orange under the hind legs. The males grow to 2½ inches long; the females, to over 3 inches.

In April the males croak in shallow ponds. The females lay masses of jelly-coated eggs in the water. The tadpoles which hatch from the eggs grow to about 3 inches long. They have dark backs, dark purplish tail crests, and are iridescent underneath. In summer the tadpoles change into frogs.

The leopard frog, or meadow frog, is a little larger than the pickerel frog. Its back is green or brownish and the rounded dark spots on it are outlined with white. Underneath it is white.

Early in spring the females lay jelly-coated eggs in masses attached to a support under water. The eggs hatch into tadpoles which grow for about three months, until they are 3 inches or longer. The tadpoles are brown with black specks on the back, light underneath, and have translucent edges on their tails. As the tadpole changes into a frog the back legs develop, then the front ones break through. The tiny tadpole mouth changes to the wide frog mouth. Although the small frog still has a tail, it can now jump out of water. After a few days the tail disappears.

Tadpole — to Frog

LEOPARD FROG

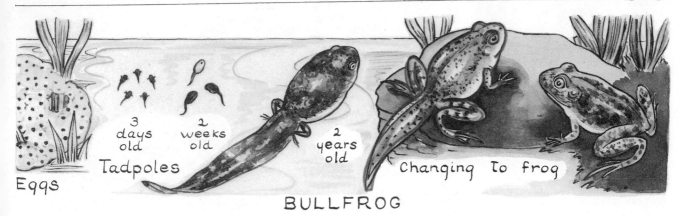

3
days
old

2
weeks
old

2
years
old

Tadpoles

Changing to frog

Eggs

BULLFROG

BULLFROG AND GREEN FROG

These frogs always live in or near water. The big bullfrogs are among the last to mate and lay their eggs. In June and July we hear the *garrumping* croak of the males in ponds and lakes. The females lay thousands of small black jelly-coated eggs. These float on the surface of the water in large masses from 2 to 5 feet across. After a few days the eggs hatch into tadpoles, which take two years to grow up. Full-grown tadpoles are from 4 to 6 inches long and are brownish splotched with black on the back and yellow underneath. They change into 1½- to 2-inch frogs which have the same coloring on the back and are white underneath. As the frogs grow, they become green on the back; males have a yellow throat in summer. The bodies of the males grow to 7½ inches long; those of the females grow to 8 inches.

Bullfrogs eat insects, worms, small frogs, crayfish, and other small animals. In the water they catch small fish.

The green frog is like a small bullfrog except for the fold of skin which goes down each side of its back instead of ending around the ear as on the bullfrog. The green frog usually has some black splotches on the back and sides. The males grow to 3½ inches long and the females to 4 inches. In June and July they lay masses of eggs on the surface of shallow water or over water weeds. In less than a week the eggs hatch. The tadpoles take two years to reach their full size of from 3 to 3½ inches. They are brownish with dark spots and creamy underneath. The second summer the tadpoles change into frogs a little over an inch long.

BULLFROG

GREEN FROG

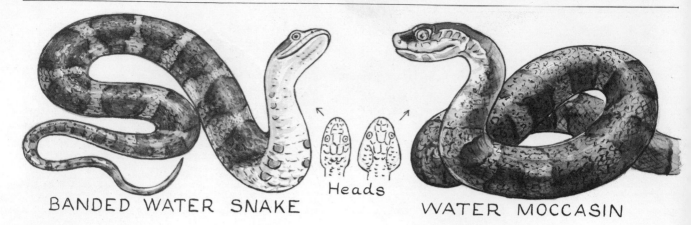

BANDED WATER SNAKE   Heads   WATER MOCCASIN

SNAKES

The banded water snake is the snake most often seen near water in the northeastern states. It is dark brown or light brown with dark bands that are broadest at the middle of the back. It grows to about 4 feet long. This snake is not poisonous, but it will coil and strike if annoyed. It catches and eats small creatures which it finds in or near water, such as fish, frogs, tadpoles, insects, and mice. Late in summer the female has from sixteen to forty-four young which she bears alive.

The water moccasin lives in the southern states and in the Mississippi Valley as far north as southern Illinois. It is often found in shallow water and marshes. It grows to 5 feet long and 10 inches around. In color it is olive-brown with darker crossbands. Because of the white inside its mouth, it is also called a cottonmouth. It eats fish, frogs, and other small animals that it finds around water. The young are born alive, from one to twelve at a time.

The water moccasin will fight if cornered; its bite is very poisonous, although it is not usually fatal.

The garter snake is sometimes found near water. It eats frogs, toads, salamanders, crayfish, and minnows, as well as insects, worms, and mice. It grows to about 3 feet long, the female sometimes being larger than the male. This snake's back is brown with three yellow stripes; underneath it is light yellowish. It is not poisonous, but it may bite and give off an odor if captured. Late in summer the female has from twelve to seventy live young, each about 6 inches long.

The ribbon snake, a close relative of the garter snake, is brighter and more slender. On the back it has three bright yellow stripes separated with dark brown; it is greenish-white underneath. Usually it lives on land near water, where it catches tadpoles, frogs, salamanders, insects, and worms. The young snakes, from 8 to 9 inches long, are born alive, usually twelve to a litter.

GARTER SNAKE

RIBBON SNAKE

(young) SNAPPING TURTLE (Adult)

TURTLES

The snapping turtle, or snapper, grows to over 2 feet long and may weigh more than 40 pounds. It is the largest turtle of the eastern states, where it lives in ponds, lakes, and streams. Its dark brown upper shell does not cover its heavy neck, legs, and long saw-toothed tail. The under shell is still smaller, which gives the legs and head room enough to move freely. When catching its food, the turtle darts its head forward and snaps with its strong jaws. It eats fish, frogs, insects, crayfish, ducklings, and other creatures, as well as some water plants.

In spring or summer the female snapper digs a hole in soft, damp earth and lays twenty or more eggs in it. The round, white, hard-shelled eggs are about an inch in diameter. They hatch in about three months into tiny turtles with long tails. Sometimes the eggs are dug up and eaten by minks, weasels, skunks, or other animals before they have a chance to hatch.

Snapping turtles hibernate in mud under water. They may live twenty-five years or longer.

The musk turtle lives in mud at the bottom of ponds and marshes. Although it is small (5 to 6 inches long) it can bite hard. It can give off such a strong musky odor that it is often called a "stinkpot." It has a smooth, arched, brown upper shell which can cover the limbs fairly well. The under shell is small and yellowish. On each side of its head it has two yellow stripes. The male can be told from the female by his longer tail.

The musk turtle eats fish, worms, insects, water plants, and garbage. It can stay under water a long time. In June the female comes out on land to lay her one to nine white oval eggs. She lays them either on the surface or underground. They hatch in two or three months into inch-long turtles.

The mud turtle also lives on the muddy bottom of ponds, sometimes in shallow water. It grows to 4½ inches long and has a dull brown upper shell. It can be told from the musk turtle by its larger under shell. This is hinged so that it can be drawn tightly against the upper shell.

(Young) MUSK TURTLE (Adult)   (Young) MUD TURTLE (Adult)

The map turtle is found in some northern rivers and lakes. It likes deep water and places where the water plants are thick. It gets its name from its olive-brown upper shell with light yellowish markings, which resemble a map. It grows to 10 inches long and may weigh over 4 pounds.

Soft-shelled turtles are odd-looking creatures which live in rivers, often staying in shallow water which has a muddy bottom. They sometimes float below the surface with their pointed snouts sticking up for air. One kind of soft-shelled turtle lives in the East, another in the South, and another in the Midwest. The chief difference among them is that some have spiny tubercles along the front of the upper shell and some do not. The shell is light brown with dark spots. It is flexible, like rubber, and is from 8 to 15 inches long. The female is the larger, although the male has a longer tail.

The only time these turtles leave the water is in summer, when they lay their eggs. The females lay from two to four sets of eggs in rather deep holes in moist sandy soil. There are from twelve to twenty-four eggs in a set. They are round, white, brittle, and a little over an inch across. They hatch in about three months into inch-long turtles whose soft shells are speckled with dark polka dots.

These turtles eat fish and other water creatures and some plant food. They sometimes grow to weigh 20 pounds or more. In the Midwest, where they are most common, they are used for food.

SPOTTED TURTLE

Spotted turtles usually live near ponds. They like to feed under water, where they eat small fish and shellfish. They also feed on land, eating earthworms, insects, snails, and berries. Their smooth, black, arched shells have bright yellow spots. The male's shell grows to 5 inches long; the female's, to 4 inches. The male's tail is longer and his eyes are brown; the female's eyes are orange, and her jaws are pale yellow.

In June the female lays from two to four eggs underground in a sandy spot. The eggs are white, oval, and a little over an inch long. The young do not hatch until September. At first they have only one yellow spot on each section of the upper shell. More spots appear as the turtles grow larger. Spotted turtles may be kept as pets since they do not bite. In captivity they will eat earthworms, raw fish or meat, and lettuce and other vegetables.

MAP TURTLE   Adult   (Young)   SOFT-SHELLED TURTLE   Adult

PAINTED TURTLE

The painted turtle always lives near water since it does all its eating under water. It helps keep the water in a pool clean as it eats almost anything it can find: insects, shellfish, snails, and other animals, either living or dead, as well as some water plants.

The shell of the painted turtle grows to 7 inches in length and is shiny olive-brown or black with yellow lines on the back and red marks along the edges. On the head it has yellow marks and on the neck and legs, red stripes. The male has long, thin nails on the front feet; the female, short stubby ones. The female turtle is over four years old when she starts laying eggs. She digs a hole in the ground near the pond and lays from four to eight white or pinkish oval eggs. In summer the eggs hatch into inch-long turtles.

Wood turtles usually live on land in the warm weather. In spring or fall they go into the water to mate, and in cold weather they go into the mud under the water to hibernate. They are also called sculptured turtles because of the deep ridges in their shells. The shells are brown with yellow and black markings and grow to about 8 inches long. The neck and the underside of the legs and tail of these turtles is brick red. The male has a longer tail and longer nails than the female. In June the female lays from two to twelve oval eggs in the sand. Wood turtles eat berries, mushrooms, leaves, insects, and small water creatures.

The box turtle lives on land, but sometimes goes into the water to cool off or to escape from an enemy. The under shell of this turtle is hinged and can be closed tightly against the upper shell to form a box with the turtle inside. The upper shell is high, rounded, and is dark brownish with yellow marks. It grows to 5 inches long. The male turtle usually has red eyes; the female, yellow or brown eyes.

In spring the female lays from three to eight oval white eggs in a small hole that she digs in a field. The eggs hatch in three months into baby turtles a little over an inch long. It usually takes these turtles five years to reach their full size. They may live more than one hundred years.

Box turtles eat plants, insects, worms, slugs, snails, and other small creatures. Sometimes they grow so fat they cannot close their shells.

(Adult) WOOD TURTLE (Young)   (Young) BOX TURTLE (Adult)

BELTED KINGFISHER

BIRDS THAT NEST NEAR WATER

Some land birds live and build their nests near ponds and streams.

Kingfishers are found near water all over the United States. The belted kingfisher is a bluish-gray and white bird that grows to 12 or more inches long. The female has a band of reddish-brown across the breast and along the sides. Both male and female have a top-heavy look with their large heads and bills, short tails and small feet. They use their strong bills to catch fish when they dive headfirst into the water.

The kingfisher's home is a tunnel in a bank. The male and female both work on the tunnel, digging with their bills and feet. At the enlarged end of the tunnel the female lays from five to eight or more glossy white eggs on the bare ground or on a layer of fishbones or other material. For seventeen days she, or sometimes the male bird, sits on the eggs. The young birds which hatch have no feathers at first and are blind for two weeks. They stay in the tunnel for about four weeks while both parents keep busy feeding them small fish. When they are older, they eat insects, crayfish, frogs, mice, lizards, and other small creatures, and also some kinds of berries.

Red-winged blackbirds live in swamps. Some stay in the South the year round. In the north-eastern states the redwings return in spring. The males come first, usually in March. Their *ok-a-lee* call rings out as they search for nesting places. When the females come later, they do all the work of nest-building.

The nest is either woven around cattails growing in water or it is placed in a low tree or bush beside the water. It is usually made of strips of reed or other stems, lined with fine rootlets. In it the female lays three or four eggs which are light blue with dark markings. She sits on them for about two weeks until they hatch. Both parents feed the young on insects for the ten days or so that they stay in the nest. Later they will all eat grain and weed seeds.

Redwings are about 9 inches long. Adult males are all black except for the red and yellow shoulder patch. Young males are streaked or brownish with orange shoulders. Females are streaked light and dark brown.

RED-WINGED BLACKBIRDS

SWALLOWS: 1) BARN; 2) CLIFF

Length: 1) 7½ inches; 2) 6 inches. Color: 1) steel-blue back, red forehead and throat, light reddish underneath; 2) steel-blue back, white forehead, reddish cheeks, buff rump, light brown underneath. Nest: 1) on wall; 2) on cliff or wall.

SWALLOWS: 1) BANK; 2) ROUGH-WINGED

Length: 1) 5½ inches; 2) 5¾ inches. Color: 1) grayish-brown on back and breast band, white underneath. 2) grayish-brown back, light brownish breast, white underneath. Nest: 1) in tunnel in bank; 2) in hole in bank, tree, or building.

WATER-THRUSHES: 1) LOUISIANA; 2) NORTHERN

Length: about 6 inches. Color: olive-gray on back. 1) whitish underneath with dark streaks; 2) yellowish underneath with dark streaks. Nest: moss, leaves, and twigs, on banks or under roots.

PHOEBE

Length: 7½ inches. Color: olive-gray on back, darker wings and tail, light underneath. Nest: mud, grass, fibers, covered with moss and lined with hair, grass, feathers. Placed in a crevice, or on wall, or under bridge or roof.

SWAMP SPARROW

Length: 5¾ inches. Color: brown and black on back, gray on head and breast, brownish-red on crown, white on throat and lower under parts. Nest: made of grass in clumps of sedge or reeds in swamp in northern and eastern states.

MARSH WRENS: 1) SHORT-BILLED; 2) LONG-BILLED

Length: 1) 4½ inches; 2) 5 inches. Color: 1) streaked brown, black, and white on back; 2) brown with black and white streaks on back, brown and black crown. Nest: woven reeds.

MALLARD FAMILY

DUCKS

Many kinds of ducks live in ponds and lakes throughout the country.

Mallards are common everywhere. They live in parks as well as in wild places, and in Europe and Asia as well as in the United States. In China mallards were used to breed the white, or Peking, ducks that American farmers raise on duck farms.

Mallards are about 24 inches long. The male, or drake, is glossy blue-green on the head and neck with a narrow white neck band; brown and gray on the back; black and white on the tail; reddish-brown on the breast, and whitish underneath. The wings have a purple band. The female is streaked light and dark brown with a purple wing band. In summer and fall, when the drake is molting, he looses his bright colors and resembles the female.

Early in spring the female makes a nest on the ground, usually under a bush or tall grass. The nest is made of fine reeds, grass, or leaves lined with down from the duck's breast. The duck sits on her six to thirteen greenish-brown eggs until they hatch in about four weeks. The ducklings are downy yellow and brown. They are soon able to run about, swim, and catch their own food.

Mallards eat all kinds of food, including tadpoles, small fish, snails, and plants.

Black ducks, both male and female, have the same general coloring as the female mallard, but they are darker and they do not have a white line bordering the purplish-blue wing band as the mallard does. Black ducks live in the northern half of the United States and in Canada in summer and along the eastern coast of the United States in winter. Their nesting habits are the same as mallards'. They eat plants and sometimes fish and mussels, often feeding at night.

BLACK DUCK

WOOD DUCK (Male)

WOOD DUCK (Female and Young)

The male wood duck is a beautiful and brightly colored bird. He is dark iridescent green on the head and back, black on the tail, reddish-brown on the breast and rump, and yellow-gray on the sides with lines of white or black separating the colors. His bill is black, white, and orange, and his eye is red. The female wood duck is a neat gray and brown with a white line through the eye. She is a little smaller than the male, which grows to 20 inches long. Both male and female have head crests.

Wood ducks live all over the United States in woodland ponds. They nest in hollow trees nearby. The female lays from eight to fifteen cream-colored eggs in a down-lined nest. She sits on the eggs until they hatch in about four weeks. The downy brown and buff ducklings stay in the nest only a day or two. Then they jump down to the ground, often a distance of from 10 to 40 feet. The ducklings take to the water at once, and look for mosquito wrigglers and other things to eat. Adult wood ducks eat mostly plant food, such as grass, seeds, nuts, roots and duckweed. They also eat some insects.

Because of hunters and the clearing of woodlands, these ducks were becoming rare. Now that they are protected by law they are increasing. Many people have put up nesting boxes to take the place of hollow trees.

Another duck that is beautifully marked, though not so gay in color, is the pintail. It can be told from other ducks by its slender neck and the two long feathers in the tail of the male. The male is reddish-brown on the head, gray, white, black, and brown on the back, white on the lower neck and underneath. He grows to about 30 inches long. The female is yellowish- and grayish-brown and has a wedge-shaped tail. These birds usually nest in the northern states and Canada. They are seen in the East when they are migrating to the South for winter.

Pintails eat grain and insects. They can dive and swim under water.

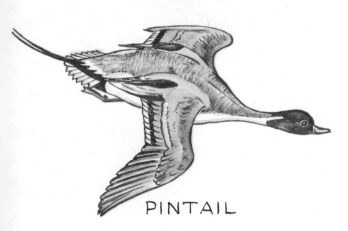

PINTAIL

MERGANSERS: 1) AMERICAN; 2) HOODED
Length: 1) 26 inches; 2) 18 inches. Color: 1) male, dark green head, black back, white body; female, gray with reddish-brown head; 2) male, black and white, reddish-brown underneath; female, gray with reddish head and crest.

TEAL: 1) GREEN-WINGED; 2) BLUE-WINGED
Length: 1) 14 inches; 2) 16 inches. Color: 1) male, reddish-brown and green head, grayish body; female, brownish; 2) male, gray and white head, brownish body, blue shoulder.

1) CANVASBACK; 2) REDHEAD
Length: 1) 24 inches; 2) 23 inches. Color: 1) male, red head and neck, black foreparts, white body; female, reddish-brown and gray; 2) male, red head, black neck and foreparts, gray body; female, brown. Nest: in northwestern marshes.

1) GOLDENEYE; 2) BUFFLEHEAD
Length: 1) 20 inches; 2) 15 inches. Color: 1) male, dark green and white head, black and white body; female, brown head, brown, gray, and white body; 2) male, iridescent black and white; female, gray and white. Nest: in hollow trees in North.

RUDDY DUCK
Length: 16 inches. Color: male, black and white head, reddish-brown body, dark brown up-turned tail, white underneath, bluish bill; female, gray and brown; young, brown and white. Nest: made of reeds and grass in northern states.

BALDPATE or WIDGEON
Length: 18 to 21 inches. Color: male, green and white head, brown and gray back, white, black, green, and brown wings, brownish-red and white underneath; female, mostly gray and brown. Nest: on ground in marshes in North. Winters in South.

CANADA GOOSE FAMILY

GEESE

The Canada goose is seen in some part of the United States in every season of the year. In autumn large flocks fly southward in V formation, often honking loudly. They stop in grain fields and meadows along the way to eat seeds, grass, berries, and roots. In spring they live in the western and northern states and Canada where they raise their families. A few may stay in the East throughout the year. The geese in the picture live near a parkway only a few miles from New York City.

Canada geese usually make their nests on the ground near water. They use grass and leaves and line the nest with down. The goose sits on her five to nine cream-colored eggs until they hatch in about four weeks. The downy yellow goslings eat grass and other plants, including dandelion stems, while both parents guard them. The family stays together until autumn when the young have their full plumage. Then they join the flock. Canada geese grow to 3½ feet long and to 18 pounds in weight. They have black heads and necks with white chin straps and brownish-gray bodies.

The brant is a smaller goose with somewhat similar coloring.

The snow goose lives in the western states and sometimes, in autumn and winter, along the eastern coast. In spring these geese travel north in large flocks which fly in a wider V than that of Canada geese. Snow geese raise their families on the flat plains of the far north. Nests are made of moss and usually hold six dull white eggs.

The snow goose is all white except for the black feathers on the tip of the wing. Its bill and feet are pinkish.

The blue goose, which often lives and sometimes mates with the snow goose, has a white head, grayish body, and some white and black on the wings.

SNOW GOOSE

BLUE GOOSE

KILLDEER and Young

WILSON'S SNIPE

FRESH-WATER SHORE BIRDS

These birds make their nests on the ground near fresh water or in marshes. They lay three or four eggs that hatch into downy young. These are able to run about soon after leaving the shell.

The killdeer is named after its call, a repeated *kill-dee*. It is a kind of plover which lives throughout the United States and makes its nest in both wet and dry places. On the back it is olive-brown; on the rump, orange-brown; underneath, white with two black bands on the breast. It grows to about 10 inches long. It eats insects, worms, crayfish, and other small water creatures.

The spotted sandpiper is the little bird (7 to 8 inches long) that we see bobbing along the edge of brooks as well as on the seacoast. It is sometimes called a "peep" or "peet-weet" because of its cry, and a "teeterer" because of its walk. It can dive into water and swim if necessary.

The sandpiper's back is grayish-brown; underneath it is white with black spots. It eats insects.

The common, or Wilson's, snipe lives in marshes in the North in summer and in the South in winter. It is about 12 inches long and is striped and mottled in light and dark brown. It has a long bill which it pokes into the mud in search of food. It eats water insects and other small creatures.

Late in spring the male bird makes a courting flight, circling in the sky while making a humming sound with his wings. In spite of its small size and usefulness, the snipe is often hunted.

The woodcock is another bird that has been hunted so much that it has greatly decreased in numbers. It is about the size of the snipe, but is more rounded in shape. In color it is mottled and striped in reddish-brown, gray, and black on the back and pale orange-brown underneath. The courting male flies in the evening, cheeping at the same time.

The woodcock lives in the eastern part of the United States in swamps and woods. It eats earthworms which it pulls up with its long bill.

SPOTTED SANDPIPER

WOODCOCK and Young

FLORIDA GALLINULE and Young

COOTS and Young

MARSH HENS or MUD HENS

These birds live among the reeds and grasses of swamps and ponds. They can walk over the mud and matted roots on their long toes without sinking in. With their bobbing heads, upturned tails, and clucking calls they resemble small hens. Their food is chiefly insects, snails, seeds, and water plants.

The marsh hens make their nests of reeds and grasses on dry ground or in a swamp. In either place the nest is well hidden under clumps of grass. Each nest holds from six to twelve or more light or dark buff-colored, spotted eggs. In two or three weeks the eggs hatch into downy black chicks which are able to run about almost at once.

The Florida gallinule is more common in the South but it also lives in northern ponds. It is dark gray with some brown on the back, a white streak on each side, and white under the tail. Its bill and forehead are bright red. It is about 14 inches long.

The coot is a plump, dark gray bird with a white bill. Its large feet have scalloped, or lobed, toes. Baby coots are black with orange hairlike feathers and a red bill. Flocks of coots live in ponds in many parts of the country. They are 16 inches long, a little smaller than the ducks that they swim among.

Rails live in many of the eastern and other states, but they are not often seen, as they hide among marsh grasses and are most active at night.

The king rail is 19 inches long. It is light olive-brown with dark streaks on the back, reddish-brown on the neck and breast, brown and white underneath. Its long bill is yellow and brown.

The Virginia rail has much the same coloring, but it is only 11 inches long.

The sora is only 9 inches long. It is olive-brown with black and white marks on the back, gray with white underneath, and black on the face and throat. Its short bill is yellow with a dark tip.

KING RAIL and Young   VIRGINIA RAIL and Young   SORA and Young

EGRET   SNOWY EGRET

HERONS

Egrets are beautiful white herons. In the past, large colonies of them lived in the southern states. During the last century many were killed for the long, graceful white plumes which they have at mating time. These plumes were used to decorate ladies' hats. Now egrets are protected by law and they are increasing in numbers. They are sometimes seen in the northern states in summer where they wander after the nesting season.

The large egret is the one most often seen in the North. It is about 41 inches long and has a yellow bill and black legs. The snowy egret is 24 inches long and has a black bill and legs and yellow feet. It has a crest instead of a smooth head.

The egrets' nest is a platform of sticks laid across the branches of a tree. It contains from three to five pale blue eggs which hatch in about four weeks. The young stay in the nest about three weeks, and both parents take care of them.

Egrets eat insects, worms, lizards, and other small creatures. They wade into the water on their long legs to catch fish.

The great blue heron, which is over 4 feet tall, is one of the larger herons. It often stands like a statue in the water with its neck curved and its eyes cast down, waiting for a fish to swim into reach. With a swift dart of its head it catches the fish in its long bill. Or sometimes it stands on one foot and catches the fish in its other foot. Sometimes it stalks through fields catching mice and other small creatures.

The great blue herons fish alone but gather into colonies, or heronries, at nesting time. The nest is a bulky arrangement of twigs, usually placed near the top of a tall tree. The same nest may be used for many years. There are from three to six bluish eggs which hatch in four weeks. The parents feed the clamoring young by coughing up fish into their bills.

This heron's coloring is more gray than blue. Its head is white, with a long black plume on either side; its back and sides are gray shading to black; its bill is partly yellow; and its long legs are gray.

The little blue heron is bluish-gray with purple on the head and neck. Before it is two years old it is white, sometimes with a bluish tinge. It is about 2 feet long and nests in the South.

GREAT BLUE HERON

GREEN HERON and Young

The green heron, which is only 18 inches long, is one of the most common of the heron family. It is greenish with gray markings on the back, dark green on the top of the head, reddish-brown on the neck, brown with some white underneath, and yellow on the legs.

The green heron runs along the edge of streams. There it hunts for fish, worms, snakes, and other small creatures. It is most active in early morning and at dusk. Its nest is a platform of twigs in a bush or tree near water. The three to six pale greenish eggs hatch in seventeen days. Sometimes a few nests may be close together, but green herons do not place their nests in a large colony.

The black-crowned night heron is from 24 to 26 inches long. It is black on the head and back, gray on the sides, and white underneath. In the evening, night, and early morning it wades in streams, catch-ing fish, frogs, and other small animals.

At nesting time the black-crowned herons gather into colonies, usually in deep woods, often some distance from water. Their loud, squawking cries are heard as they fly back and forth. The twig nests are built in trees, bushes, or on the ground. Each holds from three to six pale greenish eggs which hatch in about twenty-five days. The young are fed by both parents for three weeks or longer. They are brown streaked with white.

The bittern is a kind of heron which lives in wild ponds and marshes over much of the United States. It does not gather into colonies at any time. Usually it hides among marsh grasses where its mixed brown, black, and white coloring blends with the background. The least bittern is only 12 inches long; the large bittern is twice as long. The weird *plunk-a-lunk* cry of the large bittern is heard more often than the bird is seen.

In spring bitterns make a nest of dead rushes, usually among reeds in a swamp. The larger bittern lays from three to five brownish-gray eggs, which hatch in twenty-eight days. The least bittern lays from three to six bluish-white eggs, which hatch in seventeen days. The young birds are buff colored and fuzzy. Their long necks and bulging eyes give them an odd expression. When feeding, each young bird grabs the bill of a parent, who then coughs up some partly digested food.

BLACK-CROWNED NIGHT HERON

BITTERN and Young

COMMON LOON and Young

DIVING BIRDS

In summer, if you are near a northern lake, you may hear the weird call of a loon. The common loon is a large bird, nearly 3 feet long. It is black and white on the back and white underneath. It can dive and swim under water. When it starts to fly, it must take off from the water as it cannot balance well on land. Its chief food is fish.

Loons nest on the shore or sometimes on top of a muskrat house. Their nest is either a bare hollow in the ground or a platform of sticks and reeds. The two olive-brown, dark-spotted eggs hatch in about a month. The downy young are gray on the back and white underneath. At first they may ride on the back of a swimming parent, but soon they are able to swim by themselves.

Grebes live in lakes, ponds, and streams. They are smaller than loons and they have long necks and almost no tails. When in danger, they quickly dive or sink under water. They can rest or swim in the water with only their heads showing. Like loons, they must take off from water when they fly.

The grebe's nest is a raft of rushes or other water plants. This nest either floats on water or is anchored to a support. The eggs are dull white, cream, or brown with dark stains. There are from three to eight or more of them. In about three weeks they hatch into downy young which can swim almost at once. Sometimes the young ride on the parents' backs. The food of grebes consists of insects, snails, fish, and other water creatures.

The horned grebe is about 14 inches long, is black and buff on the head, gray on the back, brown on the breast and sides, and white underneath. It nests in the northern states and Canada.

The pied-billed grebe is the most common of the three and is found in most of the United States. It is dark brown on the back, lighter brown and white underneath, and has a black throat and a black band on its bill. It is about 13 inches long.

The western grebe is larger than the others, 24 to 29 inches long. It is black and white. In the past, many of them were killed for the thick, soft breast feathers which were used on hats.

HORNED GREBES

PIED-BILLED GREBE

WESTERN GREBES and Young

OSPREY

HAWKS

The osprey, or fish hawk, is a large bird, 2 feet long, with a wingspread of over 4 feet. It is dark brown on the back, white with dark streaks on the head, and white with some dark spots underneath. It is often seen hovering in the sky above a pond or lake. So keen is its eyesight that while it is still up in the air it is able to spy a fish in the water. It catches the fish, which is the only kind of food that it eats, by suddenly dropping to the water and grabbing it in its strong claws.

Ospreys make their nests of sticks, seaweed, or other material in trees, on the ground, or on poles. On Long Island so many ospreys nested on power-line poles that the power company put up special nesting poles for them to use. In each nest there are from two to four eggs which are dull white or buff, spotted and blotched in shades of brown. The eggs hatch in four weeks into young birds which soon have a covering of brown and buff feathers. The young stay in the nest for eight weeks while both parents bring them fish to eat. Every year the ospreys add to and use the same nest.

The marsh hawk is a little smaller than the osprey. It flies closer to the ground, winging back and forth over fields and marshes.

The male hawk is gray on the back with black wing tips, white on the rump and under parts. The female is brown instead of gray and is streaked with brown underneath.

These hawks nest in a tangle of weeds or grasses in a marsh. The nest is made of dried marsh grasses. There are usually from four to six dull white eggs in a nest. Both parents sit on the eggs for about a month, until they hatch into blind and helpless young ones.

Marsh hawks are not fish eaters like the osprey. Their diet includes small animals such as mice, squirrels, rabbits, birds, snakes, and frogs.

OSPREY NEST ON POLE

MARSH HAWK

MUSKRAT

WATER SHREW

FUR-BEARING ANIMALS

The animals shown on these pages live near water all or most of their lives.

The muskrat lives in a tunnel in the bank or in a house of mud and rushes in a pond or marsh. In either home the entrance is under water.

The muskrat looks like a large rat with a stout body and a scaly tail flattened on both sides. Its fur is thick and gray close to the body, coarse and brown on the outside. The hind legs are longer than the front ones, and the feet are partly webbed. In the water the feet are used as paddles and the tail as a rudder.

Muskrats eat the leaves and roots of water plants and some water animals. They are most active at night. Between early spring and late summer they usually have three families, with from four to six or even more babies in a family. For the first two weeks the babies are blind, but by the time they are about a month old, they are able to swim and dive and find their own food.

The water shrew is a small mouselike animal which lives in the northern states and Canada. It has soft fur which is gray on the back and white underneath the body and the long tail. Its tiny eyes and ears are almost hidden in its fur. Its hind feet are larger than its front feet and are partly webbed

and fringed with hair. By holding air bubbles in its feet, the water shrew is able to walk on the water. It is also able to swim and dive and run along the bottom of a stream. It catches and eats small fish and other water creatures.

The common shrew, smaller and more brownish than the water shrew, often hunts near streams.

All shrews are very active and eat a great deal. They have two or three families in a season, with from three to ten in each. The young are able to care for themselves when a month old. They do not live much over a year.

The star-nosed mole lives in swampy places in the northern and eastern states. It is from 7 to 8 inches long. It has soft gray fur and a fleshy fringe, or star, on the snout, and a hairy tail. Its broad front feet have strong claws with which the mole digs tunnels and swims. With its fringed nose it searches for worms, insects, and other food.

This mole is active both day and night. In spring it has its one family of the year. The three to six young are born in a nest in a tunnel, under a stump or other shelter. They are able to care for themselves when less than a month old.

STAR-NOSED MOLE

Raccoons usually live in trees near water, although they may also live in caves or burrows in dry country. The raccoon is a long-furred animal with a long tail and a stocky body. It has a black mask across the eyes, a grayish body, and black rings on the tail. It weighs from 10 to 25 pounds or more.

In spring the mother raccoon has four or five young ones in a hollow tree or other shelter. The young have soft fur and are blind for the first three weeks. They stay with their mother through the first year. As soon as they are big enough, they go out hunting with her at night. The 'coons eat almost anything, including grain, fruit, fish and shellfish, frogs, worms, insects, and mice. Sometimes they get into cornfields and chicken yards. When near water, they hold their food in their front paws and wash it before eating.

In the South raccoons are active all winter. In the North they sleep in hollow logs or dens during cold weather. Several of them may use the same winter quarters.

Young raccoons make interesting but mischievous pets. Older ones are likely to be cranky.

MINK

Minks hunt along the banks of streams and also in the water as they are good swimmers. They are long, slender animals about the size of a small house cat. Their fine, soft fur is reddish or dark brown and there is a white spot under the chin. Although their legs are short, they can travel fast by looping their slender bodies.

The mink does most of its hunting at night. It lives entirely on flesh. It catches many small animals, including rats, mice, ducks and other birds. Sometimes it kills young muskrats. In a poultry house a mink can do much damage.

The mink's home is a den in the rocks, a hollow log, a burrow under tree roots or other shelter. In spring five or six young are born. At first they are covered with short white hair and are blind for up to five weeks. Until late in summer they live with the mother. Sometimes the father stays with the family. Minks are active through the winter except in the coldest weather.

RACCOON

Beavers live in ponds and lakes. If they cannot find a suitable pond, they make one by building a dam across a stream.

The beaver is an oversized member of the rodent family. It is from 3 to 4 feet long. An old beaver may weigh from 50 to 70 pounds or even more. It has brown fur that is thick and soft next to the skin and coarser on the outside.

The beaver is an expert swimmer. Its broad, flat, scaly tail acts as a rudder, and its large webbed hind feet as paddles. It can store enough air in its lungs to stay under water a quarter of an hour. After leaving the water it combs itself dry with special claws on the inner toes of its hind feet.

The home of the beaver is a den in a bank or a lodge built in the water. The lodge is made of logs and boughs, stones, and mud. The top is always above water, and the doorways under water. The room inside is from 4 to 5 feet across and 3 feet high. One beaver family, consisting of father, mother, and two sets of young, usually lives in the lodge.

In spring, when it is time for a new family to be born, the father leaves home temporarily and the two-year-olds leave for good. The mother is left with the young of the year before and the three or four new babies. The baby beavers weigh about a pound. They have soft fur and a 3½-inch tail. Their eyes are open from the first. Before they are a month old, they are able to swim and dive.

Beavers are vegetarians. They eat water plants and roots and the leaves and shoots of land plants. In winter they live on the bark of logs they have stored under water.

The beaver cuts down trees to get logs for the winter food supply and for dams and lodges. It gnaws around the trunk with its strong teeth until the tree falls. Then it cuts the trunk and branches into logs that it can drag away. If the logs are too far from the pond, the beaver digs a canal on which to float them.

Dams are made of logs, sticks, and stones with mud and weeds stuffed into the holes. The work is done at night, with all the grown beavers in the community helping. Every year the dam is repaired and added to until it becomes very strong.

BEAVER FAMILY

OTTER FAMILY

Otters are long, sleek animals with soft, thick, dark brown fur. They are from 3 to 4 feet long and weigh from 10 to 25 pounds. The female is smaller than the male. Otters live near streams and lakes in wild country in most of the United States.

The otter is more at home in water than on land. With its long body, webbed feet, flat head, and strong tail it can dive, swim, and wriggle through the water.

The home of the otter is a burrow in a bank, an abandoned beaver den, a hollow under a tree, or some other shelter along the shore. In April the young otters are born, one to five in a family. At first their eyes are closed and their fur is dark brown or black. When they are five weeks old they open their eyes. Soon after that the mother takes them out and teaches them to swim and to fish. At first they sometimes ride on her back. The family stays together for about a year, until it is time for the next family.

The otter's favorite food is fish, which it is an expert at catching. It also eats shellfish, insects, frogs, salamanders, and sometimes muskrats and young beavers, as well as ducks and other birds. In winter it catches fish in open streams or through holes in the ice.

All the otters, young and old, seem to like to play. Their favorite sport is sliding down a slippery mud or snow bank. Folding their legs under their body, they "belly whop" into the water.

There are a great many creatures and plants which live in or near ponds and streams. Some of them you will not find anywhere else; others you will sometimes find in dry places. Many creatures which live on dry land come to the water when they are thirsty. If you watch beside a pond or stream you will learn a great deal about wild life and growing things.

Other books which tell about plant and animal life in ponds and streams are listed on page 72.

INDEX

MORE TO READ

BIRDS

Audubon Water Bird Guide, by Richard H. Pough (Doubleday)

Birds of America, by T. Gilbert Pearson (Garden City)

Ducks, Geese and Swans of North America, by F. H. Kortright (Stackpole)

Field Guide to the Birds, by Roger Tory Peterson (Houghton)

FERNS

Ferns, by Farida A. Wiley (American Museum of Natural History)

Field Book of Common Ferns, by Herbert Durand (Putnam)

FISHES

Book of Fishes (National Geographic)

Fisherman's Encyclopedia, ed. by Ira N. Gabrielson (Stackpole)

North American Game Fishes, by Francesca La Monte (Doubleday)

Northern Fishes, by Samuel Eddy and Thaddeus Surber (University of Minnesota)

Representative North American Fresh-Water Fishes, by John T. Nichols (Macmillan)

FLOWERS

Beginner's Guide to Wild Flowers, by Ethel H. Hausman (Putnam)

Field Book of American Wild Flowers, by F. Schuyler Mathews (Putnam)

Wild Flower Guide, by Edgar T. Wherry (Doubleday)

FROGS AND SALAMANDERS

Handbook of Frogs and Toads, by Anna A. and Albert H. Wright (Comstock)

Handbook of Salamanders, by Sherman C. Bishop (Cornell University)

Reptiles and Amphibians of the Northeastern States, by Roger Conant (Zoological Society of Philadelphia)

INSECTS

Field Book of Insects, by Frank B. Lutz (Putnam)

Insect Guide, by Ralph B. Swain (Doubleday)

Junior Book of Insects, by Edwin Way Teale (Dutton)

MAMMALS

Animal Book, by Dorothy and Nils Hogner (Oxford)

Field Book of North American Mammals, by H. E. Anthony (Putnam)

Mammals of North America, by Victor H. Cahalane (Macmillan)

SNAKES AND TURTLES

Field Book of Snakes of North America and Canada, by Karl P. Schmidt and D. Dwight Davis (Putnam)

Reptiles and Amphibians of the Northeastern States, by Roger Conant (Zoological Society of Philadelphia)

Reptiles of North America, by Raymond L. Ditmars (Doubleday)

Turtles, by Wilfrid T. Bronson (Harcourt)

Turtles of the United States and Canada, by Clifford H. Pope (Knopf)

GENERAL

Beginner's Guide to Fresh-Water Life, by Leon A. Housman (Putnam)

Book of Wild Pets, by Clifford Moore (Putnam)

Field Book of Ponds and Streams, by Ann Morgan (Putnam)

Fieldbook of Natural History, by E. Laurence Palmer (McGraw)

In Woods and Fields, by Margaret Waring Buck (Abingdon)

Life of Inland Waters, by James G. Needham and J. T. Lloyd (Comstock)

Wildlife in Color, by Roger Tory Peterson (Houghton)

NATURE BULLETINS

The National Audubon Society, 1130 Fifth Ave., New York City, publishes many nature bulletins at ten cents each. Many states also have free or inexpensive publications on trees, shrubs, flowers, birds, mammals, reptiles, and insects. You can write to your state museum, state conservation department, or state department of education at your state capital, for a list of their nature publications.

MAGAZINES

Audubon Magazine, published by National Audubon Society, New York City

Junior Natural History, published by American Museum of Natural History, New York City

National Geographic Magazine, published by National Geographic Society, Washington, D. C.

Natural History, published by American Museum of Natural History, New York City

Nature Magazine, published by American Nature Association, Washington, D. C.

Outdoors Illustrated, published by Canadian Nature, 188 Jarvis Street, Toronto, Canada